AROUND
THE
M25

AROUND THE M25

John Burke

HALE · LONDON

© *John Burke 1986*
First published in Great Britain 1986

ISBN 0 7090 2795 8

Robert Hale Limited
Clerkenwell House
Clerkenwell Green
London EC1R 0HT

British Library Cataloguing in Publication Data

Burke, John, *1922-*
    Around the M25 : a guide to more than
    200 beauty spots just off the motorway.
    1. London Orbital Motorway Region
    (England)—Description and travel—
    Guide-books— I. Title
    914.22'04858   DA 670.S63

ISBN 0-7090-2795-8

Photoset in North Wales by
Derek Doyle & Associates, Mold, Clwyd.
Printed in Great Britain by
St Edmundsbury Press Ltd, Bury St Edmunds, Suffolk.
Bound by Woolnough Bookbinders Ltd.

CONTENTS

LIST OF MAPS

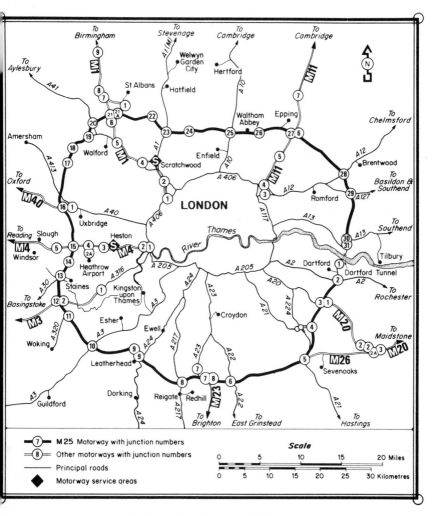

The M25 London Orbital Motorway

LIST OF ILLUSTRATIONS

Illustrations by Sue Scullard

1 INTRODUCTION

INTRODUCTION

Completion of the London Orbital Motorway, the M25, has brought a wealth of delightful countryside within easy reach of drivers from London and the Home Counties. It is now far less harassing for residents east of the metropolis to visit friends and relatives, or simply to explore open spaces and historic sites, to the west without the need to edge a slow way through congested city streets. The same is of course true of north-to-south travel, or indeed of any combination of directions.

This book aims to draw attention to easily accessible open spaces, woodlands, country parks, forest trails and many other leisure amenities within reasonable range of the M25. One's own starting point will obviously affect what might be considered 'reasonable'; but by and large I have tried to keep to a pattern of easygoing day trips for the family which involve no more than an hour's drive from the selected M25 junction, and in most cases no more than thirty to forty-five minutes. Due allowance has been made, as far as possible, for differences in travel conditions between one region and another: the same mileage can take twice as long to cover along, say, some Kent and Sussex minor roads as along a fast west-bound motorway. At the same time, while such motorways make it practicable to reach some quite distant places within the allotted hour and even within half that time, the emphasis here is on having an enjoyable day out with the family rather than on speed and endurance tests.

The region covered has been divided up into seven sections, starting with Junction 1 of the M25 in the south-east, where it emerges from the Dartford Tunnel, and working round to the final junction in the north-east at the entry to that tunnel. (No purely eastern division is feasible, since the River Thames widens out in that direction to occupy a large part of any conceivable map.) Within each chapter the sequence of trips has been arranged from the numbered succession of M25 exits, with sites grouped according to their relative nearness to those exits. Some interesting places on the extreme fringes of the different regions are mentioned at the end of the chapter or section for the benefit of those who are in the mood to go just a little bit further; but even these few recommendations are little more than an hour's journey.

In many cases it is simple to go from one park or picnic place to another along the same route, and return to a different junction if so desired. Such possibilities are noted where applicable, and where there are alternative approaches from either of two junctions these are also mentioned. This makes for a more logical progression than purely alphabetical lists; but readers wishing to look up the name of a specific site can do so in the index.

At the time of going to press, a few sections of the motorway are still not fully operational, and it may be that more convenient exit roads may be introduced than I have been able to verify at present, but the general suggestions should not be seriously affected.

Most of the open spaces dealt with are freely accessible to the public. In the case of some country parks and locally administered woodlands there may be a car-park fee. No attempt has been made to specify these: prices vary from place to place and from year to year, and may also vary seasonally; but the charge is usually a nominal one, and every over-taxed motorist nowadays is accustomed to such imposts! Only where there is some special charge is this mentioned. In all other cases it can be assumed that entry to the area is free.

The National Trust and English Heritage issue their own guides to properties under their jurisdiction, and there are several other guides to museums, stately homes and private properties open at various times to the public. This present publication does not intend to duplicate these. Nevertheless, it would be rather silly not to draw attention to some particularly notable house or castle within a few minutes of the open space being visited, so where relevant a brief note has been added to the main reference. The letters NT signify the National Trust; AM, an Ancient Monument in the care of English Heritage – or, to give it its full title, the Historic Buildings and Monuments Commission for England. The majority of such properties ask an admission fee. As these vary even more widely than car-park charges, they too will be omitted from these pages.

They can be checked in advance in the publications of the organizations concerned.

Also the National Trust, like the Forestry Commission, administers many woodlands in the interests of conservation and of appreciative visitors. Rather than refer to their involvement in each relevant entry in this book, I have done so only when there is a particular reason for expanding on the subject. Since 1972 their work has been supplemented by the admirable Woodland Trust, established to combat the wanton destruction of so much of our rural heritage. It tries to preserve the original character of old woodlands while at the same time offering scope for informal recreation, though without too much in the way of public car-parks and other facilities which might clash with the natural surroundings.

A number of public open spaces and footpaths adjoin, or are incorporated with, National Nature Reserves under the care of the Nature Conservancy Council. In general the Council welcomes interested visitors who respect its main purpose of conservation. Many Reserves have a warden who will be happy to give advice and explain any local restrictions designed to protect wildlife. Leaflets, nature trails and observation hides are provided at certain locations.

In a book such as this, which invites people to enjoy to the full our national heritage of field and woodland, ancient tracks and historic sites, it is more than ever important to emphasize the need to protect such treasures for the benefit of others. It cannot be said too often that the Country Code should be strictly observed, not just in Nature Reserves but across the whole landscape:

Guard against all risk of fire.
Fasten all gates.
Keep dogs under proper control.
Keep to the paths across farm land.
Avoid damaging fences, hedges and walls.
Leave no litter – take it home.
Safeguard water supplies.
Protect wildlife, wild plants and trees.
Go carefully on country roads.
Respect the life of the countryside.

To this might well be added the injunction printed on Trosley Country Park leaflets: Take nothing but pictures; leave nothing but footprints; kill nothing but time.

JUNCTIONS

2-5

Sites described in this chapter are nearly all in Kent, with an occasional foray over the border into Sussex or the south-eastern fringes of Greater London, and are reached largely with the help of other motorways across the county. Away from the industrial tangle of the North Kent bank of the Thames, and only a few minutes off those motorways, there are still orchards and hop gardens, secretive little villages and surviving tracts of the once vast forest which in Roman and early Saxon times covered the entire Weald.

Stretches of the North Downs Way and Pilgrims' Way (also referred to in Chapters 3 and 4) cross the region and offer spectacular views from the Kent Downs, classified as an Area of Outstanding Natural Beauty. Anyone fancying a long or short walk can pick up the footpaths at any of several roadside points, identified by an acorn waymark on a low stone plinth or the occasional wooden signpost.

There is also the Saxon Shore Way, a linkage of coastal paths into a long-distance route from Gravesend to Rye. At times it deviates inland to follow roughly the coastline of Roman times, passing the ruined Roman forts of the Saxon Shore.

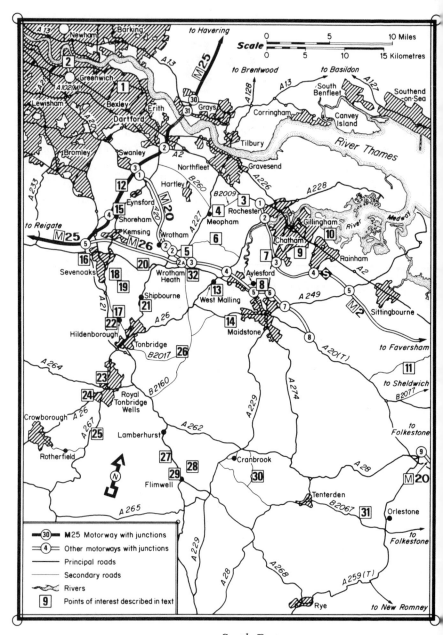

South-East

Key

1	Abbey Wood, Erith
2	Greenwich Park
3	Shepherds Gate Picnic Site, near Chatham/Rochester
4	Camer Country Park, Vigo
6	Holly Hill Wood, near Vigo
7	Bluebell Hill Picnic Site, near Chatham/Rochester
8	Cobtree Manor Country Park, Aylesford
9	Capstone Farm Country Park, near Chatham/Rochester
10	Eastcourt Meadows Country Park, near Gillingham
11	East Kent Country Tour
12	Lullingstone Park, Eynsford
13	Manor Park Country Park, West Malling
14	Teston Bridge Picnic Site, near Maidstone
15	Andrews Wood, Badger's Mount, near Shoreham
16	Dryhill Picnic Park, near Sevenoaks
17	Hollanden, near Hildenborough
18	Knole Park, Sevenoaks
19	One Tree Hill, near Sevenoaks
20	Oldbury Hill and Styants Wood, near Wrotham
21	Dene Park, near Shipbourne
22	Barnetts Wood Picnic Site, near Tonbridge
23	Hurst Wood, Tunbridge Wells
24	High Rocks, near Tunbridge Wells
25	Nap Wood, near Rotherfield
26	Whitbread Hop Farm, Beltring
27	Bewl Bridge Reservoir, near Lamberhurst
28	Bedgebury Forest and National Pinetum, Flimwell
29	Pillory Corner Picnic Site, Flimwell
30	Hemstead Forest, near Cranbrook
31	Faggs Wood, Orlestone
32	Heart of Kent Country Tour

FROM JUNCTION

2

1 ABBEY WOOD, Erith

Take westbound A2 towards London. At Bexley roundabout turn right on A220 towards Erith, then left on A206 by Erith parish church. The cool woodlands are flanked by grassy slopes, with the picturesque ruins of Lesnes Abbey at the heart of it all.

2 GREENWICH PARK, Greenwich

Take westbound A2 towards London. From the airy expanse of Blackheath common, once a haunt of highwaymen but now criss-crossed by roads, there is an entrance to the park, with a drive sweeping down to the northern gate. The steep slope above the River Thames commands a wonderful view of dockland and, in the distance, St Paul's, Tower Bridge and a forest of skyscrapers. Within the spacious parkland with its oak, chestnut and hawthorn are the Royal Observatory, the meridian marker establishing 'Greenwich time', the Royal Naval College, the National Maritime Museum and the Queen's House, designed by Inigo Jones for Anne of Denmark, wife to King James I.

A short distance from the northern edge of the park are the towering masts of the famous tea clipper the *Cutty Sark* and, dwarfed by its mighty neighbour, *Gipsy Moth IV*, in which Sir Francis Chichester sailed round the world single-handed. A squat rotunda nearby marks the entrance by lift to a pedestrian tunnel under the Thames to the Isle of Dogs, where a pleasant little park offers a panoramic view of the Greenwich waterside's most magnificent buildings.

3 SHEPHERDS GATE PICNIC SITE, near Chatham and Rochester

Take eastbound A2 towards Rochester. At the Cobham/Shorne interchange the picnic site is signposted south of the main road beside B2009 but is so sheltered that it is not immediately obvious.

One must swing right round onto the approach marked Golf Club, and there under the over-arching trees is a picnic site with a small formal car-park and other parking spaces in the leafy shade. WC.

On the opposite side of B2009 are the seventy-eight acres of Ashenbank Wood, an area of mixed broadleaved woodland with a number of paths and rides, surprisingly quiet in spite of the A2 traffic close to its northern edge. There are some fine large specimens of mature oak, cherry, sweet chestnut and beech trees. The wood is easily reached on foot from the picnic site, but there is also parking in a layby beside B2009, and roadside parking is permitted in the lane running parallel with the A2.

NEARBY FEATURES:

Cobham Hall, on B2009 at northern entry to Cobham village. A sixteenth-century and later mansion, in whose large park Charles Dickens took his last walk. Now a girls' school, but open to the public over Easter weekend, a few days in late July, and Wednesday, Thursday, Sunday and Bank Holiday Monday afternoons in August. Fee. Teas available. WC.

Owletts (NT). At south end of Cobham village. A red-brick house from the time of Charles II, with a fine staircase and plasterwork, spacious garden and orchard. Open Wednesday and Thursday afternoons April to October. Fee.

4 CAMER COUNTRY PARK, near Meopham

Follow directions for preceding entry, then continue southwards on B2009. The country park is signposted to the left on a sharp bend on the outskirts of Meopham.

Here are forty-six acres of undulating parkland, basking in a designated Area of Outstanding Natural Beauty, with graceful clumps of trees, picnic tables, benches and seats at intervals. Old tree stumps and warped, monstrous branches trailing along the ground simply ask to be clambered over and treated as make-believe dragons. Through the trees to the north, seemingly a whole world away, can be glimpsed the chimneys and industrial haze of Gravesend. WC.

An alternative approach is to turn south off the A2 slightly earlier than beside the Shepherds Gate picnic site, onto A227 signposted

Meopham and Trosley Country Park, then turn left in Meopham on
B2009 signposted Cobham.

NEARBY FEATURES
Meopham Green, south of Meopham on A227, has a huge
village green with a long tradition of local cricket dating from
1778. Behind the Cricketers inn stands an 1801 smock mill,
restored in 1962 and open on Sunday afternoons in July and
August.

5 TROSLEY COUNTRY PARK, Vigo

Follow directions for preceding entry, then continue southwards on
A227 and follow signs through Vigo village to Trosley Country
Park. There are picnic tables and benches near the main car-park
entrance. Parking is also allowed beside some of the woodland trails
themselves. WC.

The park consists of an extensive and varied area of woods and
rolling downland, open daily from 9 a.m. until dusk except for
Christmas Day. Adjoining the car-park at the entrance is a visitors'
information centre, open Saturday, Sunday and Bank Holiday
afternoons. When it is shut there is a dispenser of waymarked walk
leaflets close at hand, and large display boards with maps and
information. The North Downs Way and the Pilgrims' Way, in
partnership here as along so much of their routes, cut right through
the site.

Visitors can picnic and wander freely through 160 acres of
woodland and meadow beside meandering streams, or follow paths
out of the woods up the chalk escarpment of the Downs. For those
with time and energy to spare, three waymarked routes offer a
choice between $3\frac{1}{2}$ and seven miles through and beyond the
confines of the park, designated the Harvel Hike, the Trosley
Ramble and the Coldrum Trail. It is possible – and very rewarding –
to try at any rate a part of these walks and then take a short cut back
to base.

Alongside two of the suggested trails stand the Coldrum Stones,
one of a number of neolithic tombs found around the valley of the
River Medway. This long barrow, some four or five thousand years
old, once consisted of a closed burial chamber at the eastern end of

an earthen mound surrounded by twenty-four sarsen stones, of which only four still remain upright. Some bones removed from the barrow are displayed in the porch of Trottiscliffe church nearby, a Norman building on a Saxon site. The name Trosley is in fact a corruption of the old village name of Trottiscliffe.

Whitehorse Wood consists mainly of chestnut coppice, developed to provide poles for the now dwindling hop gardens and for local fencing. Here and there in the landscape may be seen oast-houses, the conical-roofed ovens in which hops were dried for use in brewing, though all too many of them nowadays have been converted into private dwellings as their old functions had to be abandoned.

Yew trees are prominent on the scarp of the Downs, happy on the surface chalk but with their dark shadows inhibiting the growth of other trees or plants. The name of one section of the Harvel Hike tickles one's curiosity: Wrangling Lane. It is believed to derive from the old use of this route by complainants taking their grievances to the lord of the manor at Luddesdown or Buckland.

Alternative approach: from M25 junction 3 take eastbound M20 towards Maidstone, turn off at M20 junction 2 to roundabout and then take northbound A227 and follow Country Park signs.

6 HOLLY HILL WOOD, near Vigo

This is incorporated in one of the longer walks from Trosley Country Park (see preceding entry) but can also be reached by road from M2 junction 2. Turn south on A228 to Snodland crossroads, there turn right (west), and after about 150 yards, where the road turns left, continue straight on for a mile and a half. At T-junction turn right up Birling Hill, and on the crest of the Downs turn right up Holly Hill to large car-park on the left.

On one of the highest peaks in Kent, these thirty-two acres of wooded nature reserve combined with public open space offer sweeping views across the Downs and the valley of the River Medway.

7 BLUEBELL HILL PICNIC SITE, near Chatham and Rochester

Take eastbound A2 towards Rochester and continue on M2 to M2 junction 3. Turn south on A229 towards Maidstone and into Common Road opposite the Upper Bell inn. Open daily 9 a.m. to dusk except Christmas Day. WC.

The parking plateau on the crown of the ridge offers one of the most breathtaking views in south-east England, over the Medway valley, taking in Maidstone and Aylesford, and successive ridges and hills, with the South Downs like a cloud line in the distance. Overgrown quarries make strange, twisted hollows in the ground shelving steeply away below. Cloudy day or sunny day, there is always a wealth of colour and contrast.

The North Downs Way skirts one edge of the site and provides a walk of about three-quarters of a mile to Kit's Coty House (AM, open to inspection free at all times). This most impressive of the neolithic tombs scattered in the neighbourhood was once a large earthen barrow, of which only three large stones remain like a miniature section of Stonehenge.

A few hundred yards south is Little Kit's Coty, sometimes referred to as the Countless Stones because, however many times its jumbled fragments are counted, they never seem to add up to the same number and it is hard to establish where one begins and the next finishes.

8 COBTREE MANOR COUNTRY PARK, Aylesford

Take eastbound A2 towards Rochester and continue on M2 to M2 junction 3. Turn south on A229 towards Maidstone. Just beyond junction with M20 take minor road to right, signposted Aylesford. The country park is on the right. WC.

Greensward and little plantations, with plentiful benches and tables informally scattered over the undulating area, lead up to deeper woodland on the steep slopes of a ridge north of Maidstone, interwoven with footpaths and bridleways for pony trekking.

An alternative approach is from M25 junction 3. Follow M20 towards Maidstone. At M20 junction 6 turn right on southbound A229 towards Maidstone, then follow minor road to the right as described above.

NEARBY FEATURES:
On the other side of the minor road into Aylesford, before

reaching the country park, is the spacious open-air museum of Kent Rural Life, with a reconstructed oast-house, displays of farming history and equipment, and plans to develop orchards and a typical Kentish market garden. Open April to mid-October, daily. Fee. WC.

A lane beside the museum leads to a lock and bridge over the River Medway, with riverside walks and an entrancing prospect of moated Allington Castle, in the keeping of the friars of Aylesford's Carmelite friary and open every afternoon except Christmas Day.

9 CAPSTONE FARM COUNTRY PARK, near Chatham and Rochester

Take eastbound A2 towards Rochester and continue on M2 to M2 junction 3. Turn north on A229 towards Chatham. Turn right into Walderslade Woods, second left into Fostington Way, right into Princess Avenue, and on to North Dene Way. Turn right into Capstone Road, and the park entrance is on the right. WC.

There is an unspoilt stretch of downland here on the fringe of the busy Medway townships, with a variety of flora and fauna. A coarse-fishing lake is open daily from dawn to dusk.

NEARBY FEATURES:
Rochester's wide grassy riverside below the castle has ample space for picnics, with seats and a view of Medway shipping. Norman keep of castle (AM) has an entrance fee, but its grounds and the walks down to the riverside are free. River trips from Strood Pier and the Paddle Steamer Preservation Society at Chatham Historic Dockyard. There are frequent open days and steam weekends at Chatham Dockyard Railway.

10 EASTCOURT MEADOWS COUNTRY PARK, near Gillingham

Take eastbound A2 through Rochester and on towards Gillingham. In Gillingham turn north on B2004 through Lower Rainham. A mile east of the Strand is a car-park at Sharps Green entrance to sixty acres of natural riverside meadows, ideal for walking and picnicking – a great place, too, for studying birdlife and the traffic of the Medway estuary.

NEARBY FEATURES:

Matthew's International Equestrian Centre. At Walnut Tree Farm, Lower Rainham Road, is one of the most extensive riding centres in Britain. Indoor arena, stables, shop, restaurant. Visitors are welcome free. WC.

Sittingbourne. At Dolphin Yard off Crown Quay Lane (signposted from town centre and ring road) are preserved some of the great Thames and Medway sailing barges, with a traditional sail loft and a museum display. Open Sundays and Bank Holidays from Easter to mid-October, also Saturday afternoons in July. The Sittingbourne and Kemsley Light Railways runs steam services from a station beside Milton Road (also lavishly signposted) on Sunday afternoons from Easter to October; Wednesday, Thursday and Saturday afternoons during August, and Bank Holidays.

11 EAST KENT COUNTRY TOUR

This begins virtually on the eastern limit of our eastbound spur along the A2 and M2, but one starting point is comfortably within an hour's run from M25 junction 2 and is well worth considering for a day's picturesque rural drive. It is at its best in spring, when the orchards of 'the Garden of England' are in blossom.

The tour can be picked up at Sheldwich on A251, south of M2 junction 6. It follows a roughly circular route of about fifty miles over the North Downs and Wealden countryside, signposted in an anti-clockwise direction by a white tree symbol on a brown background.

Just beyond Challock is King's Wood, fourteen hundred acres of hardwood, conifers and sweet chestnut, with forest clearings in which deer can occasionally be seen. Among the nature trails is one $2\frac{1}{4}$-mile walk waymarked through the woods.

There is limited parking beside a nature reserve on Wye Downs, offering wide-ranging views to the south. Where the route picks up Stone Street, B2066, near Lyminge is West Wood, 440 acres of woodland with a picnic place and a $2\frac{1}{2}$-mile waymarked walk. WC.

Soon after the route swings westward, back towards its starting point, we reach Howlett's Zoo Park near Bekesbourne (admission fee), open daily except Christmas Day. Just before Selling are Perry Wood and Selling Wood, 150 acres criss-crossed by footpaths, with plenty of picnic spaces. Rabbits, badgers and foxes run wild in woodland which owes its unspoilt character to the fact that it was owned for centuries by Corpus Christi College, Oxford, being taken over by the local council only in 1980. There was once a wooden semaphore tower at the highest point, now rebuilt as a vantage point and dubbed 'The Pulpit'.

Local Automobile Association offices provide a free leaflet covering a similar route to the above.

FROM JUNCTION

3

12 LULLINGSTONE PARK, Eynsford

Take eastbound A20 towards Maidstone, then past roundabout take southbound A225 through Eynsford. Just beyond the entrance gates to Lullingstone Castle turn right along road signposted Lullingstone Park and Golf Course. Beyond Castle Farm turn sharp right to car-park half a mile up the hill.

There are three hundred acres of parkland and woodland with nature walks, bridlepaths and plenty of space for picnics. Also a public golf course and a restaurant. WC.

NEARBY FEATURES:

Lullingstone Castle. Set in its own gardens below the park, the castle is a mainly eighteenth-century house with a splendid Tudor brick gatehouse. Open Saturday, Sunday and Bank Holiday afternoons April to October. Fee.

Lullingstone Roman Villa (AM). Remains of a large villa with fine mosaics under protective roofing, incorporating a gallery of archaeological exhibits and interesting details of pagan and Christian worship existing side by side.

13 MANOR PARK COUNTRY PARK, West Malling

Take eastbound M20 towards Maidstone. Leave M20 junction 4 on southbound A228 towards Tonbridge. The fifty-two-acre park is just south of West Malling, overlooked by a distinguished manor house and the spire of the local church above the trees. A fine place for games and picnics, the site includes a lake, little plantations, clumps of great trees, and a succession of grassy ridges and hummocks. Logs and fallen trees provide natural adventure playgrounds, with one play-log area for children close to the car-park. Open from 9 a.m. to dusk daily except Christmas Day. WC.

There are four waymarked walks starting within the park and leading out across the countryside: Woods Meadow Walk (three miles), the Millstream Walk ($3\frac{1}{2}$ miles), St Leonard's Walk (four miles) and the Quintain Walk ($4\frac{1}{2}$ miles).

The first leads past a cascade built under a Gothic arch in 1810 by the then owner of St Mary's Abbey, on whose ruined ragstone walls grows marjoram toadflax, sometimes called Malling toadflax. It is believed to have been introduced by a Spanish nun many centuries ago and to grow nowhere else in England except on the walls of Wells Cathedral in Somerset. A little further on, Banky Meadows are reputed to have provided the burial site for those dying of the Black Death in the fourteenth century. The route then passes through Woods Meadow at Leybourne, where picnic sites are set in wooded glades beside the stream. This public open space of Woods Meadow can also be reached from the A20 just west of Maidstone.

The Millstream Walk makes its way through orchards and watercress beds past oast-houses and timber-framed dwellings characteristic of the Kentish Weald, including the Barracks and Cobbs Hall, farmhouses of the sixteenth and seventeenth century respectively.

St Leonard's Walk crosses the main road close to a gaunt Norman tower built as a fortified home by Bishop Gundulf, Bishop of Rochester and designer there of the early castle and cathedral. Nearby are fragments of a small chapel. In its time the Norman keep has served as a prison and a hop store. More recent, but still of some age, is the seventeenth-century Ryarsh Mill, once working as a flourmill driven by Leybourne stream.

The Quintain Walk is named after the jousting target on Offham village green, the only one of its kind surviving in England. It is made up of a post carrying a rotating beam on a pivot, with a target board at one end and a sandbag at the other. Horsemen tilted at the target with lances and, if they scored a good blow, had to dodge the sandbag as it swung back at them. This same walk leads through Moorlands Wood, rich in bird and wild flower life.

Those wishing to see the quintain without the effort of making the walk can do so by driving southwards on the A228 and taking the first right turn along a minor road to Offham.

Alternative route to Manor Park: from M25 junction 5 take the eastbound M26 and then M20 to M20 junction 4, and A228 as above.

NEARBY FEATURE:
Great Comp Gardens, Borough Green. Off B2016, reached from Manor Park by road through Offham. Private gardens beautifully conceived and developed by the owners of the early-seventeenth-century house which provides a focus for the patterns of trees, shrubs, heather, lawns and plants. The house itself is not open to the public, but the gardens are open daily (fee), 11 a.m.-6 p.m., April to October. Garden centre. Refreshments Sundays and Bank Holidays only.

14 TESTON BRIDGE PICNIC SITE, near Maidstone

Take eastbound M20 towards Maidstone. Leave M20 junction 4 on southbound A228 towards Tonbridge. Turn left on A26 and right on B2163. Entrance to the site is on the right between the level crossing and the river. Beside a fine medieval stone bridge over the Medway are twenty-four acres of nice rough open space, with tables and benches dotted here and there. WC.

There is a lock busy with river craft, and unspoilt views up a gentle slope from the far bank to a smart trio of black-coned, white-cowled oast-houses. This is a good starting place for towpath walks towards Tonbridge or Maidstone, through quiet scenes of orchard, woodland and a few surviving hop gardens.

Teston Bridge is one of the attractions on the Heart of Kent Country Tour (see end of chapter).

NEARBY FEATURE:

Boughton Monchelsea Place. From Teston, continue along
B2163 and turn right on A229. The house is a castellated
Elizabethan and Regency manor, with noble views across its deer
park and the Kentish Weald. Open Good Friday until October
on Saturday, Sunday and Bank Holiday afternoons, and on
Wednesday afternoons in July and August. Fee.

FROM JUNCTION

4

15 ANDREWS WOOD, BADGER'S MOUNT, near Shoreham
Take A21 signposted Bromley. At roundabout follow A224 to
Badgers Mount, and at next roundabout minor road signposted
Shoreham. A quarter of a mile along on the right is car-park for
Andrews Wood, 185 acres of mixed woodland with a picnic area
and an interesting one-mile walk.

FROM JUNCTION

5

16 DRYHILL PICNIC PARK, near Sevenoaks
Take southbound A21 and turn right at roundabout onto A25. A
quarter of a mile along the road, turn left by signpost to picnic site
and car-park.

The area was once a quarry for Kentish ragstone, a hard sandy
limestone underlying much of this neighbourhood. It was used as
far back as Roman times, especially for road- and wall-building, and
shipped in large quantities to London via the Medway and the
Thames: one load was rediscovered in 1962 in a sunken barge near
Blackfriars, with a coin dated AD 89 in the mast instep. There are
some interesting rock formations to be seen here, set in twenty-two

acres of grassland and new woodland. A large shelter, welcome during unexpected showers or outbreaks of blustery wind, has been provided with tables and benches for picnics. An information leaflet is obtainable at the entrance. Open 9 a.m. to dusk daily except Christmas Day. WC.

17 HOLLANDEN, near Hildenborough

Take southbound A21. South of Sevenoaks turn left on B245 towards Hildenborough. Hollanden is signposted from B245 at the Mill Garage, Hildenborough.

This is a finely maintained survival centre with more than fifty different breeds of rare farm animals on display in a natural countryside habitat. There is a pets' corner, and the woodland trail features a stream and a millpond. 'Pick your own' fruit and vegetables from mid-June until late September.

Open daily 10.30 a.m-6 p.m. from 1 May until 30 September. Entrance fee, with reductions for children and OAPs. WC.

18 KNOLE PARK, Sevenoaks

Take southbound A21. At interchange take eastbound A25 into Sevenoaks. Near railway station turn right on southbound A225 through the town to Knole Park. The great deer park is open daily, free, for pedestrians only: cars are allowed in only when carrying paying visitors to the house.

There are some thousand acres to be explored, with a great open space at the heart of beech, chestnut and oak plantations. The deer are tame enough to come and beg for titbits. A good over-all view of the huge mansion can be had from Echo Mount, a hillock to the north of the park.

The house itself (NT), originating in 1465 and lived in since 1603 by the Sackville family, has important collections of silver, tapestries, furniture and portraits, including works by Reynolds and Gainsborough. Open 11 a.m.-5 p.m. Wednesday to Saturday and on Bank Holidays from April to the end of October. Fee. The garden is open the first Wednesday in each month from May to September. Fee. WC.

Alternative route, avoiding most of Sevenoaks town centre: take southbound A21 to second interchange near Sevenoaks Weald, then northbound A225 towards Sevenoaks and Knole Park.

19 ONE TREE HILL, near Sevenoaks

From either of the approaches in the preceding entry take eastbound minor road at River Hill, skirting the southern edge of Knole Park. Turn right at crossroads for parking below One Tree Hill. There are about thirty-five acres of hilly woodland, with sylvan views to the south. On the summit there was once a Romano-British burial ground.

20 OLDBURY HILL and STYANTS WOOD, near Wrotham

Take southbound A21 and then eastbound A25 through Sevenoaks. About three miles beyond the town is a parking and picnic site to the left of the road.

Rising more than six hundred feet above sea level, the hill's 150 acres are clad in beech, birch and oak woodland. Originally part of an Iron Age hill fort from about 100 BC, the height was later refortified by a Belgic tribe. One can easily pick out the encircling rampart and ditch on the south side. To the east there are views towards the Downs, and an ancient track leads up through a deep cleft from the hamlet of Oldbury, past remains of Stone Age cave dwellings in the rock.

Alternative approach, avoiding Sevenoaks town centre: take M26 towards Maidstone, and at M26 junction 2a turn south on A20 across Wrotham Heath and then right on westbound A25 through Borough Green, beyond which the parking and picnic site will be found on the right of the road.

NEARBY FEATURES:

Ightham Mote (NT). Off A227 about 2½ miles south of Borough Green. A picturesque medieval manor set in a deep vale, with a stream which has been adapted to supply a lake, the house's tranquil moat and a fishpond. The drive beside the moat is a public right of way and gives idyllic views of the house. Open every Friday afternoon and on Sunday afternoons April to September, but plans are in hand to extend opening hours to five days a week. Fee.

Old Soar Manor (NT and AM). Off A227 along a narrow lane two miles south of Borough Green. The surviving solar block of a thirteenth-century knight's residence. Open all year, on application to the key keeper. Small admission fee.

21 DENE PARK, near Shipbourne

Take M26 towards Maidstone, and at M26 junction 2a turn south on A20 across Wrotham Heath and then right on westbound A25 through Borough Green. Turn left on southbound A227 and continue through Shipbourne, whose vast village green is a playground in itself. About a mile and a half south of the village is an awkward four-way junction. Turn sharp left on minor road signposted Plaxtol.

Access to Dene Park on the left of this road is not clearly marked and not obvious until one is right upon it, so the driver should be prepared for a swift left turn into the gravelly car-park.

This is one of many scattered woodlands making up Shipbourne Forest. On its two hundred acres of coniferous and broadleaved plantations, young oak and Norway spruce grow side by side, and there are also beech, sweet chestnut, Douglas fir, Corsican pine and Japanese larch. A forest trail leads from the picnic area through woodlands and grassy rides, with a number of attractive viewpoints along the way; and there are several other easygoing footpaths from which to choose.

NEARBY FEATURES:
Ightham Mote and Old Soar Manor, as in preceding entry.

22 BARNETTS WOOD PICNIC SITE, near Tonbridge

Take southbound A21 towards Hastings. Some four miles south of Sevenoaks is the eight-acre picnic site of Barnetts Wood, a welcome refuge to the left of the main road with trees, grass and plenty of parking space.

NEARBY FEATURE:
Penshurst Place. Reached via A26 from interchange south of

Tonbridge and then the westbound B2176. Birthplace of Sir Philip Sidney. Magnificent chestnut-beamed Great Hall, furnished state rooms and a toy museum. Extensive Tudor gardens with a leisure area, adventure playground and nature trail. Open every afternoon except Monday (but open Bank Holiday Mondays) from Easter until early October. Fee. Refreshments. WC.

23 HURST WOOD, Tunbridge Wells

Take southbound A21 towards Hastings. At interchange south of Tonbridge take southbound A26 through Southborough. Minor roads past church and schools just north of the golf course lead to Hurst Wood, in a small valley on the edge of Tunbridge Wells's suburban sprawl.

Much of the timber was felled before the Woodland Trust took over administration of the area in 1983, but there are healthy recent growths of birch, oak, beech and willow. A small stream running through the woodland has never been known to dry up, even in times of severe drought. In the spring a large spread of the forty-two acres is drowned in lakes and rivulets of bluebells.

A well-maintained footpath runs through the woods and can be joined by other footpaths from both north and south.

24 HIGH ROCKS, near Tunbridge Wells

Take southbound A21 towards Hastings. At interchange south of Tonbridge take southbound A26 into Tunbridge Wells. Leave the town on minor road through Hungershall Park towards Groombridge. On the left are the slopes of High Rocks, the most substantial of the freakishly eroded formations which crop up all around Tunbridge Wells. Open daily 9 a.m. until dusk, featuring a scenic walk, hanging rocks, a rhododendron maze and plenty of open space for picnics. Small entrance fee.

Between this same minor road and the southbound A26 to Crowborough are a number of by-roads and footpaths through the woodlands and undergrowth of Broadwater Forest; and a little way south of Groombridge station is a parking place for the Forestry Commission woodlands of Harrison's Rocks.

25 NAP WOOD, near Rotherfield

Take southbound A21 towards Hastings. At interchange south of
Tonbridge take southbound A26 into Tunbridge Wells, and then
southbound A167 through Frant. Four miles south of Tunbridge
Wells is an area of more than a hundred acres of fine Wealden oak,
leased by the National Trust as a nature reserve to the Sussex Trust
for Nature Conservation. There is a permanent signposted walk
through the woods, incorporating an Iron Age trackway which
probably served the earliest ironworks in the Weald.

26 WHITBREAD HOP FARM, Beltring

Take M26 towards Maidstone. At M26 junction 2a turn south
across Wrotham Heath on A20 towards Maidstone, then right on
southbound B2016 and B2015 towards Paddock Wood. On the
right of the road at Beltring, quite impossible to miss, is the most
magnificent group of Victorian oast-houses – the largest complex of
its kind in the world.

There is an entrance fee to the Whitbread Hop Farm, but its
thousand acres do genuinely offer a whole day out for the family,
with children's pet and play areas, picnic site, shire horses on display
and a nature trail. The oast-houses and galleried barns contain
exhibitions of hopping over the years, rural crafts and agricultural
machinery.

Open 10 a.m.-5.30 p.m. Tuesdays to Sundays and Bank Holiday
Mondays, from early April to late October. Refreshments. WC.

27 BEWL BRIDGE RESERVOIR, near Lamberhurst

Take southbound M21 towards Hastings. Just beyond Lamberhurst
on A21 the reservoir is signposted to the right.

Beside the main car-park is a Visitor Centre explaining the main
features of the reservoir and its surrounding area, covering 770 acres
in all. As in so many cases when valleys have to be flooded in order
to meet demands for public water supplies, many traces of local
history disappeared below the surface; but before the job was
finished, the Department of the Environment co-operated with the
Society for Post-Medieval Archaeology and with Kentish experts on
recording excavations of forges and other ironworking equipment –

hammers, wheel pit, anvil and hearth – surviving from the busy industry of the sixteenth to eighteenth centuries in the valley.

Today a patch of woodland shelters an adventure playground, and there are several picnic places near the water. Two trails through the woods and along the banks begin at the Visitor Centre, with a number of WCs at regular intervals. Special events such as morris dancing and wildlife exhibitions are held on certain summer weekends. A little passenger steamer plies across the lake daily between April and October, with some weekend trips during the rest of the year.

Daily permits are available from the Fishing Lodge for fly fishing and boat hire, with season tickets for those likely to stay in the region any length of time. Purchase of a day permit entitles the holder to a day's membership of the Bewl Bridge Club, which has a first-floor lounge and buffet in the Activities Centre. On the ground floor are changing-rooms with lavatories and showers.

The reservoir is one of the most productive trout fisheries in the country and offers one-day fishing instruction courses on prior application to the Manager, Bewl Bridge Reservoir, Lamberhurst, Kent.

NEARBY FEATURES:
Bayham Abbey (AM). Picturesque ruins of gatehouse, chapter house, sacristy and church of a small thirteenth-century abbey set in tranquil meadows by the little River Teise. Fee. Open standard AM times, April to September.

Lamberhurst Priory Vineyards. Beside the village green on the site of medieval monastic vineyards. Visitors are welcome to the vineyard trail and wine-tastings (small fee), and conducted group tours can be arranged by prior appointment. WC.

Owl House Gardens. A turning off the northbound A21 out of Lamberhurst leads to the gardens and woodland walks of a sixteenth-century cottage named after the 'owlers' or wool smugglers who used an owl hoot as their signal. Open daily (with occasional Tuesday and Thursday closures). The owner, the Marchioness of Dufferin and Ava, donates the small entrance fees to her home for arthritics. WC.

Scotney Castle (NT). Entrance close to Bewl Bridge Reservoir entrance, on far side of A21. Gardens open from April to the end of October on Wednesdays, Thursdays and Fridays; and Saturday, Sunday and Bank Holiday afternoons. Fee. Access to the castle itself, a fairytale tower reflected in a moat, is between May and August only. WC.

28 BEDGEBURY FOREST and BEDGEBURY NATIONAL PINETUM, near Flimwell

Follow directions for Bewl Bridge Reservoir in preceding entry. Then continue towards Flimwell on A21 and turn left on northbound B2079, signposted for the Pinetum. There is a large car-park for the forest and the pinetum to the right of the road. WC.

The forest covers more than two thousand acres, with a forest walk waymarked from the car-park. Beside it are the 160 acres of Bedgebury National Pinetum, open daily 10 a.m.-8 p.m. or dusk. A small fee is payable for entry, but the spaciousness of woods and gardens is worth every penny of it.

The coniferous plantations were established in 1924, when the administrators of Kew Gardens decided to set up an outdoor laboratory in an atmosphere cleaner than that of London. In conjunction with the Forestry Commission they have developed a large estate not only of conifers but of ferns, rhododendrons, little streams and walks through green glades and beside a lake. There is a shop, and refreshments are available at weekends and on Bank Holidays.

29 PILLORY CORNER PICNIC SITE, Flimwell

Leave on southbound A21 towards Hastings. Beyond Lamberhurst and just past the turn-off to Bedgebury National Pinetum (see preceding entry), the picnic site is signposted to the right. Benches and tables are enclosed in an attractive little stockade of rustling trees, sheltering the visitor from the breeze. WC.

It is believed that the name comes from a pillory and stocks which once stood beside the main road where it is joined by B2079. Local people claim that as late as 1937 some fragments could still be identified.

From the picnic site there is a gleaming view over Bewl Bridge Reservoir.

30 HEMSTED FOREST, near Cranbrook

Take southbound A21 towards Hastings. At Lamberhurst take eastbound A262 through Goudhurst to Cranbrook. Beyond the small town (which has a visitors' information and local craft centre, and one of the most splendid smock mills in the country), turn right off A227 at Sissinghurst onto a minor road signposted Benenden. Two miles south of Sissinghurst is access to a car-park whose Forestry Commission noticeboard is almost lost in the trees at the entrance. Drivers need to proceed slowly, looking out for a sharp left turn towards Biddenden, with the parking space almost immediately on the left under a tall palisade of whispering larches. Beyond are a thousand acres of other varieties of woodland, together with a picnic site.

NEARBY FEATURE:

Sissinghurst Castle (NT). A Tudor manor house with extensive gardens laid out by Harold Nicolson and his wife, Victoria Sackville-West. The unique White Garden of white, silver and grey flowers, ferns and trees is considered by many connoisseurs to be the most beautiful garden in all England.

Open Tuesday to Friday afternoons; and Saturdays, Sundays and Good Friday 10 a.m.-6.30 p.m. from Easter to mid-October. Closed all Mondays, including Bank Holidays. Fee. Refreshments. WC.

31 FAGGS WOOD, Orlestone

Strictly speaking, this is a little way beyond the absolute fringe of our region – not so much in distance as in timing, since the absence of fast roads and the complexity of minor roads make the journey longer than it might otherwise be. Nevertheless, if one is in the region it can be reached through agreeable countryside from the M20/A20 to Ashford and the southbound A2070, or through Lamberhurst (as in preceding entries) onto A262 and B2067.

Certainly Faggs Wood can provide a welcome, cool, shaded oasis on the way to or from the Channel ports, with its 350 acres of woodland, picnic area and 2½-mile waymarked forest walk with dazzling views over the Weald towards Tenterden.

NEARBY FEATURE:
Kent & East Sussex Railway. After the closure of 'the Hoppers'
Line' which once carried so many hop-pickers from London's
East End along the Rother valley, local enthusiasts reopened a
section of the track for steam services beginning at, and returning
to, Tenterden Town station. Museum, station refreshment car,
shop, preserved locomotives and rolling-stock on station sidings.
WC.

32 HEART OF KENT COUNTRY TOUR

This and a route recommended by the Automobile Association as a
West Kent Orchards Tour (free leaflet available from local AA
offices) cover much the same territory, providing a tour of about
thirty-five miles. Kent County Council mark their chosen route
clearly on signposts. It can be picked up at the M26/A20
interchange at Wrotham Heath, from where it takes in Beltring
Hop Farm, Horsmonden, Marden, Teston and many other beauty
spots, including a number of the more interesting sites listed in this
chapter.

```
┌─────────────────────────┐
│      JUNCTIONS          │
│   5-13                  │
└─────────────────────────┘
```

Inevitably there is some overlap of routes between south-east, south and south-west, and a few sites could equally well be described on the edge of one sector or another: the English countryside is not as neatly and arbitrarily sub-divided as map-makers would wish it. In general, however, this chapter covers parts of Kent and Surrey close to London, yet happily shielded from too much turmoil, and some of the most enchanting byways of Sussex. There are also open spaces in London itself, now made accessible from approaches which could never have been contemplated only a few years ago.

From time to time the traveller will encounter stretches or the roadside markers of various major footpaths across the region, offering a change from sitting at the steering wheel. Some start outside its boundaries but have become an essential part of it.

The Wealdway, officially opened in 1981 in Ashdown Forest, begins at Gravesend and crosses both the North and South Downs, with the Weald in between. Three almost equal sections end at Tonbridge, Uckfield and Eastbourne.

A stretch of the Greensand Way was opened in 1982 between Haslemere in Surrey (an area dealt with in Chapter 4) and Limpsfield on the Kent and Surrey border, with Leith Hill at its highest point. It is hoped eventually to extend the track past Maidstone and Ashford to join up with the Saxon Shore Way at Hythe.

The Vanguard Way, devised in Footpath Heritage Year, 1980, runs from Croydon over the North Downs and through Ashdown Forest to meet the sea at Seaford.

With the aid of the M23 motorway it is in fact possible for drivers, too, to reach the coast well within the hour; but it is not the purpose of this book to discuss such obvious venues as Brighton and Worthing — there are far more tempting, quieter places to either side.

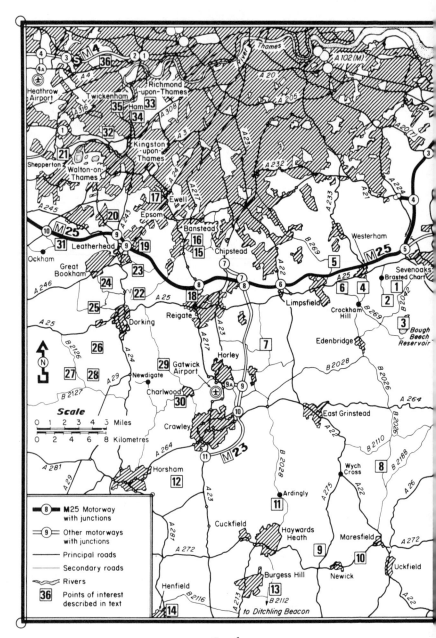

South

KEY

1   Ide Hill and Goathurst Common, near Sevenoaks
2   Toy's Hill, Brasted Chart
3   Bough Beech Reservoir
4   Westerham and Crockham Hill
5   Titsey Estate
6   Limpsfield Common
7   Outwood Common, near Gatwick
8   Ashdown Forest
9   Chailey Common
10 Piltdown Picnic Site
11 Wakehurst Place Garden, near Ardingly
12 St Leonards Forest, near Horsham
13 Ditchling Common Country Park, near Burgess Hill
14 Woods Mill, near Henfield
15 Chiphouse Wood, Chipstead
16 Banstead Commons and Banstead Wood
17 Horton Country Park, near Ewell
18 Reigate Hill
19 Ashstead and Epsom Commons
20 Oxshott and Esher Commons
21 Walton-on-Thames and Shepperton
22 Box Hill, near Dorking
23 Headley Heath, near Leatherhead
24 Bookham and Banks Commons, Great Bookham
25 Ranmore Common, near Dorking
26 Abinger Common, near Dorking
27 Holmbury Hill, near Dorking
28 Leith Hill, near Dorking
29 Prestige Wood, Newdigate
30 Glover's Wood, Charlwood
31 Ockham and Wisley Commons
32 Bushy Park, near Kingston-upon-Thames
33 Richmond Park
34 Ham Common
35 Marble Hill Park, Twickenham
36 Osterley Park

1 IDE HILL and GOATHURST COMMON, near Sevenoaks

Take southbound A21 towards Hastings. At interchange take westbound A25 towards Redhill, and in Sundridge turn left on southbound minor road. At Ide Hill there is a parking space serving the wooded tracts and footpaths of Hanging Bank and Goathurst Common, and limited parking also beside the minor road across the Common.

Ide Hill has thirty-two acres of wooded hillside overlooking the Weald, and from here and its neighbouring slopes one gets inviting glimpses of Bough Beech Reservoir a couple of miles to the south.

NEARBY FEATURE:

Emmetts Garden (NT). Reached from Ide Hill up northbound minor road towards Sundridge and Brasted. Five-acre garden with unique collection of rare trees and shrubs, set in over a hundred acres of woodland and farmland. Garden only open to the public 2 p.m.-6 p.m. Tuesday, Thursday and Sunday afternoons April to the end of October. Fee.

2 TOY'S HILL, Brasted Chart

Take southbound A25 towards Hastings. At interchange take westbound A21 towards Redhill, and in Brasted turn left on southbound minor road through Brasted Chart. There is a parking space beside the road just before entering Toy's Hill.

This car-park is in a converted gravel pit beside about a hundred acres of heath and woodland, including the height of Toy's Hill Beacon. Crowning the greensand ridge are fine beeches, some of them pollarded, and on the lower slopes there are oak, birch and Scots pine. Part of the hill has been designated a Site of Special Scientific Interest because of its wealth of plants and bird life. A short track is provided for the use of visitors in wheelchairs.

For centuries the hill was part of the 'Chart', or local

commonland, on which folk grazed their cattle and pigs and gathered fuel for their homes. There used to be woodcutters and charcoal-burners at work here, but now all is still. There was also, once, a manor house with landscaped gardens overlooked by a terrace. It came down in 1939, leaving only the overgrown terrace and patches of once-cultivated gardens.

One footpath leads through another 103 acres known as the Octavia Hill Woodlands in memory of the social reformer who in 1895 was one of the founders of the National Trust.

Alternative approach: from Ide Hill (as in preceding entry) continue south and south-west on B2042, and at T-junction turn northwards on minor road to Toy's Hill.

NEARBY FEATURE:

Chartwell. Take narrow westbound minor road from Toy's Hill and turn right at T-junction. Home of the late Sir Winston Churchill, in nearly eighty acres of parkland. Two rooms have been rearranged as a museum, but the rest, including his garden studio, are much as they were in his lifetime. Open 11 a.m.-4 p.m. Wednesday and Saturday in March and November; Tuesday to Thursday afternoons from beginning of April until end of October, plus Saturday, Sunday and Bank Holiday Mondays 11 a.m.-5 p.m. Fee. At the height of the summer season numbered tickets are issued, but visitors can pass the waiting time in the gardens. WC.

Alternative approach to Chartwell: take southbound B2026 from Westerham village on A25, and fork left after about a mile and a half.

3 BOUGH BEECH RESERVOIR

Take southbound minor roads from Ide Hill or Toy's Hill (see preceding entries) through Cooper's Corner to Bough Beech. The reservoir has a car-park, an information centre, footpath and viewing points. Fishing and Nature Reserve by permit only.

4 WESTERHAM and CROCKHAM HILL

Take southbound A21 towards Hastings, then turn right on

westbound A25 to Westerham. The little market town itself is a designated Conservation Area, and now that the weight of through traffic has been shifted to the M25 it makes an ideal centre for exploring the hills and valleys around.

Crockham Hill Common, off B2026 south of Westerham, is an extensive birch wood with wide clearings and a pleasant interlacing of footpaths. The village green at Crockham Hill is dedicated to the memory of Octavia Hill, and the doughty preserver of our countryside herself lies in the nearby churchyard, while the church itself houses an impressive recumbent sculpture of her. Mariners Hill, administered by the National Trust, is among other tracts of woodland on the greensand ridge, well served by paths, best seen at bluebell time.

NEARBY FEATURES:
Chartwell (see earlier entry for Toy's Hill).
Quebec House, Westerham (NT). A sixteenth/seventeenth-century house with relics of General Wolfe, who once lived here. Open 2 p.m.-6 p.m. daily except Thursday and Saturday, April to October; March, Sundays only. Fee. No parking except for NT members. WC.
Squerryes Court. Late seventeenth-century manor house owned by the same family for 250 years. Attractive grounds with azaleas and rhododendrons around a lake can be visited separately for a reduced fee. Open 2 p.m.-6 p.m. Saturday, Sunday and Bank Holiday Mondays March to October; also Wednesdays, May to September. Fee. Picnic site. Teas at weekends. WC.

Alternative approach: from M25 junction 6 take southbound A22 past Godstone and at roundabout take eastbound A25 to Westerham.

FROM JUNCTION

6

5 TITSEY ESTATE

Take southbound A22 past Godstone and at roundabout take eastbound A25 towards Westerham. At Limpsfield traffic lights, turn left on B269 through village. Where the road forks, turn left along Water Lane and back under the motorway. At next junction turn right through Lodge House gates to a car-park on the left.

A waymarked walk from the car-park climbs the North Downs and runs through deciduous and coniferous plantations, with seats at intervals along the route. A table map identifies distant landmarks. Birds and small animals abound, there is a badger sett, and wild plants and orchids are to be found in profusion. A rope walk descends the slope again to join the Pilgrims' Way running through the estate. The full walk covers about four miles but can be broken halfway with a return down Pitchfont Lane to the car-park.

The mansion of Titsey Place is not open to the public, but the woodland walk is open daily, free, 10 a.m.-4 p.m. from Easter Sunday to the end of October. There are two nearby picnic sites, one at Cronklands Wood, Limpsfield Chart, and the other at the junction of White Lane and B2024.

6 LIMPSFIELD COMMON

Take southbound A22 past Godstone and at roundabout take eastbound A25 through Oxted towards Westerham. On both sides of the main road at Limpsfield are acres of heath and woodland rolling from Surrey into Kent, consisting of Limpsfield Common itself, West Heath, The Chart, Little Heath and Moorhouse Bank Common, with roadside parking.

NEARBY FEATURE:

In Limpsfield churchyard are buried the composer Frederick

Delius and his wife; and Beatrice Harrison, who in the early days of broadcasting played her cello in the woods to persuade a nightingale to sing.

Alternative approach: from junction 5 take southbound A21 towards Hastings, then turn right on westbound A25 through Westerham to Limpsfield. It is in fact difficult to separate Limpsfield Common from those in preceding entries.

7 OUTWOOD COMMON, near Gatwick

Take southbound A22. In Godstone turn right on westbound A25. At Bletchingley turn right on minor road to Outwood.

Of more than two thousand acres of the Harewood Estate administered by the National Trust, the area of Outwood Common is freely open to the public, with footpaths through other parts of the woodlands. Beside the broad village green leading onto the common is the country's oldest working post mill, dating from 1665, the survivor of two mills which once operated side by side here. Its grounds, in which ducks and various animals wander at will, include a picnic site, a shop selling, among other things, flour ground in the mill, a small museum and a collection of old coaches. Small entrance fee. Open Sunday afternoons from Easter Sunday until the last Sunday in October. WC.

NEARBY FEATURE:

Gatwick Zoo and Aviaries, Charlwood. From Outwood take minor road westwards, turn south on A23 through Horley towards Brighton. Cross A217 at roundabout onto minor road to Charlwood. The zoo houses hundreds of animals and different species of birds. Squirrel monkeys rove freely (sometimes mischievously) through the grounds and mingle with visitors. Picnic site and refreshments. Open daily 10.30 a.m.-6 p.m. (or dusk) Easter to October. Fee. WC.

Alternative approach to zoo: from M25 junction 8 take southbound A217 and turn right on minor road to Charlwood (as above).

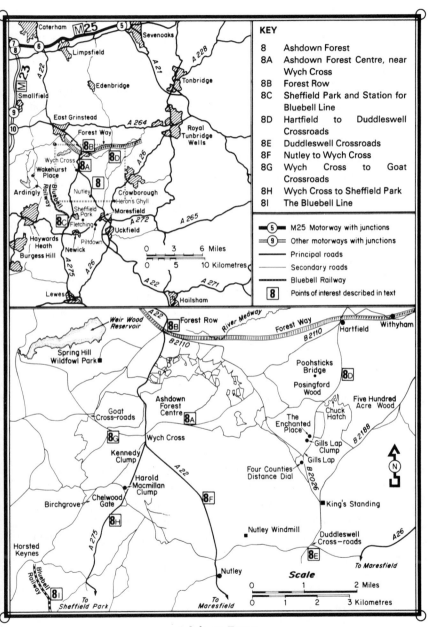

KEY

8	Ashdown Forest
8A	Ashdown Forest Centre, near Wych Cross
8B	Forest Row
8C	Sheffield Park and Station for Bluebell Line
8D	Hartfield to Duddleswell Crossroads
8E	Duddleswell Crossroads
8F	Nutley to Wych Cross
8G	Wych Cross to Goat Crossroads
8H	Wych Cross to Sheffield Park
8I	The Bluebell Line

5 — M25 Motorway with junctions
9 — Other motorways with junctions
— Principal roads
— Secondary roads
— Bluebell Railway
8 — Points of interest described in text

Ashdown Forest

8 ASHDOWN FOREST

It is impossible to split into neat segments these rolling seven thousand acres of heath and wooded commonland, rising to more than seven hundred feet out of the Sussex Weald. At the same time, one cannot deal with them in a brief single entry. Drivers with time to spare will enjoy meandering about the side roads and lanes and discovering new beauties for themselves. All we can do here is offer a few pointers to picnic and parking sites within one of the most rewarding regions in southern England.

What remains of the ancient Wealden forest, now dotted with small settlements but still rich in wide areas of common whose freedoms are jealousy guarded by the Conservators, lies roughly in a triangle between East Grinstead, Tunbridge Wells and Uckfield. Although still called a forest, it has in fact lost the majority of its trees, used long ago as fuel for the Wealden iron industry which began even before the Romans arrived, flourished in Tudor times, especially in the manufacture of cannon, and did not decline until the late seventeenth and eighteenth centuries. Names from this industrial past crop up evocatively down many a lane: Limekiln Wood, Furnace Farm, Cinder Bank ...

Apart from this despoliation, the land did not change its character, as so much of England did, because of intensive farming. None of it has ever been under the plough. A large area was for long a royal hunting forest, which gave rise to a different sort of place-name – Boarshead, Hindleap, Buckhurst and Hartfield. Later, commoners grazed their animals on it and cut the bracken and heather. Today a tricky balance is maintained between preservation of the essential character of the heathland flora and fauna and the opening-up of leisure facilities which will not damage that character. Free car-parks and informal picnic sites have been provided in abundance along most of the roads over the heath; footpath guides are readily obtainable, and on the fringes are several notable gardens and country houses.

From M25 junction 6 take the southbound A22 and bypass East Grinstead towards Eastbourne. One enters the forest proper at Forest Row, a busy, large village for long the administrative centre of the Conservators; but for a newcomer the best introduction is to be found a few miles down the road near Wych Cross.

8A Ashdown Forest Centre

Just before the main road divides opposite the Roebuck hotel into roads to Lewes and Eastbourne, a minor road branches off eastwards to Coleman's Hatch and Hartfield. A short distance along this on the left, set within tiny display plantations of characteristic local plants, an information barn is open weekends and Bank Holiday afternoons, also on weekday afternoons during the summer announced weekly on the board at the entrance – an arrangement necessitated by the fact that it is staffed largely by local volunteers. There are changing exhibitions mounted in collaboration with other local organizations, as well as a basic visual guide to the story of the forest. Maps and footpath guides are on sale here.

Beside the Centre is a large car-park with plenty of adjoining grass and scrub for picnics. Along the Ridge Road towards Coleman's Hatch are half-a-dozen similar parking spaces on both sides of the road, all commanding uninterrupted views north and south, with footpaths plunging through the bracken and climbing to clumps of sentinel trees on the skyline.

At the Centre itself begins the waymarked Broadstone Trail, for a while skirting Broadstone Warren and its large Scout camp. It cuts through woodland and over the heath, down fire rides and past an abandoned quarry from which sandstone was once extracted to build local houses. Now its contours are masked by birch trees. Along the route there are streams red with the iron which once made this an industrial heartland, crossed by a plank bridge at one point and a typical earthen-surfaced 'sod bridge' of the neighbourhood at another. There are bogs, peat, sandy hillocks and sudden vistas of the North Downs. In summer the great tracts of purple moor grass make a glowing carpet as far as the eye can see.

8B Forest Row

Retracing our steps – or tyre marks – to the cheerful bustle of the substantial village with its banks, shops and jovial inns, we have several options for exploration.

Beside the church is a road signposted Spring Hill Wildfowl Park. Taking this, one can follow further signs to the park. Its collection of cranes, flamingos, geese, swans and ducks was begun in the early 1970s and now amounts to some thousand birds living beside a fifteenth-century farmhouse once known as Mudbrooks

Farm because of the springs or brooks which provided the present lakes for the birds' habitat. Fee. WC.

From the park there is a wide panorama of Weir Wood Reservoir's gleaming expanse below. The reservoir itself is open for fishing, sailing and bird-watching only by prior permit.

Back in Forest Row, there is a large free public car-park beside the Foresters Arms inn, a short distance down the eastbound B2110 from the village hall and church towards Coleman's Hatch. WC.

Beside this car-park a wooden noticeboard points down a side lane towards the Forest Way. A more attractive stroll to join this can be taken across the green with its playing-fields and children's playground immediately opposite the car-park, swinging round to join the lane near a clubhouse and warehouses on the site of the old railway station. The track of the railway which once ran between East Grinstead and Groombridge has now been converted into a wide walk, with wider spaces at intervals to rest, picnic or just contemplate scenery which, like that of so many old railway cuttings and embankments, is shielded from everyday interruptions and clamorous neighbours. Along its route the inimitable architecture of branch-line stations is still recognizable at Hartfield and Withyham; but there is no adequate parking space at either of these two, and Forest Row is probably one of the best entry points for the walk.

NEARBY FEATURE:
Standen (NT). Reached from Forest Row by continuing on minor road around Weir Wood Reservoir from Spring Hill Wildfowl Park, or signposted off minor road a mile south of East Grinstead. A graceful Victorian house designed by Philip Webb around a medieval yeoman's house, with many wallpapers and textiles designed by William Morris. Terrace and hillside lawns and gardens overlooking Ashdown Forest. Open 2 p.m.-5.30 p.m. Wednesday, Thursday, Saturday and Sunday April to October. Fee. Refreshments. WC.

8C Forest Row to Hartfield and Withyham
As an alternative to pacing out the Forest Way path, one can drive a roughly parallel course along B2110. There are several indications along the way that one is approaching the country in which A.A. Milne lived and wrote his tales of Christopher Robin and his pets: a

house and a parking space both called Piglets, for example, and the Pooh Corner Stores in Hartfield.

At Withyham, Buckhurst Park is the private home and estate of Earl de la Warr, but a public footpath from beside the Dorset Arms hotel runs past the church and across the parkland into Five Hundred Acre Wood or on to Chuck Hatch. The wood can also be reached from B2118 between King's Standing and Friar's Gate (see next section).

8D Hartfield to Duddleswell crossroads

To the right of the B2026 about half a mile south of Hartfield is a footpath by Catchford Farm leading to Pooh Bridge, rebuilt in 1979 from the 1907 original where the game of 'Pooh Sticks' was devised and immortalized by A.A. Milne. The track continues through Posingford Wood and follows the road a while towards Chuck Hatch, then turns south to 'the Enchanted Place' situated, according to the author, 'on the very top of the Forest called Galleons Lap' – in fact, near Gill's Lap. A plaque on a large stone within a fenced-off area commemorates Milne and his celebrated illustrator, E.H. Shepard.

The large car-park at Gill's Lap on the junction of B2026 and a minor road to Coleman's Hatch offers another compelling forest viewpoint: those not wishing to walk all the way along Milne's memory lane can drive along B2026 from Hartfield, with numerous parking spaces including one for the Enchanted Place, and make a shorter stroll back to – or, indeed, in any other direction from – Gill's Lap.

Continuing on the southbound B2026 one comes to the Four Counties car-park and distance dial. Further still, past more car-parks and viewpoints, is the clump of trees and picnic benches on King's Standing, one of the highest, airiest points in the forest. Its name derives, traditionally, from the days of the royal hunting forest when Edward II, staying at Nutley hunting lodge, used this high ground as a vantage point to which herds of deer were driven by his beaters so that he could enjoy the killing without too much exertion. The hollow ways of smugglers' packhorse trails, common throughout the forest, can be traced over King's Standing; the same men bestowed the name of Beggars' Bush at Duddleswell, where they hid their cargoes in enclosures of trees and bushes.

The right fork of the junction, the B2188, leads back to Five Hundred Acre Wood (see preceding section).

8E Duddleswell Crossroads
A steely copse of radio masts rears above the crossroads, with a scattering of parking and picnic places all around, some in the direction of Crowborough, even more beside the road signposted to Nutley. One of the many footpaths leads to Nutley windmill.

8F Nutley to Wych Cross
The northbound A22 from Nutley takes us back between more parking and picnic sites to Wych Cross.

8G Wych Cross to Goat Crossroads
This road starts from the junction whose eastbound road took us to Ashdown Forest Centre. Westbound, it skirts Hindleap Warren, with parking and picnic spaces on both sides of the road, and one at Goat Crossroads, all linked by footpaths and bridleways.

8H Wych Cross to Sheffield Park
Where the southbound road forks by the Roebuck hotel, take the right-hand fork, A275, signposted Lewes. There is a parking space tucked away in the woods on the left a little way from the fork, and another on the right between the fork and Chelwood Gate. Two recent famous names are commemorated along a fire ride running parallel with the road: Harold Macmillan Clump, near Lord Stockton's home at Birchgrove, and Kennedy Clump, in memory of the US President who stayed with Macmillan shortly before his assassination. A memorial tablet on Forest Row village hall was dedicated by Macmillan in 1964.

8I The Bluebell Line
Between secluded Horsted Keynes and Sheffield Park station beside the A275 runs one of the best-known preserved railway lines in the country, providing regular daily steam services throughout the holiday season and limited services off-season, along a restored five miles of track which once formed part of the route between East Grinstead and Lewes, closed down by British Rail in 1958. There is a large free picnic site beside the car-park at Horsted Keynes station.

At Sheffield Park station, Victorian in style and in its old advertisements and name plates, the collection of veteran locomotives and rolling-stock is lovingly maintained, refurbished and added to whenever possible. Here also there is a picnic site. Refreshments. WC.

NEARBY FEATURE:
Sheffield Park Garden (NT). On the east side of A275, about half a mile north of Bluebell Railway terminus. The two hundred acres of woods, formal and informal gardens and winding paths surround five lakes constructed by 'Capability' Brown for the first Earl of Sheffield, who took his title from the local manorial estate of Sifelle. At their best in spring and early autumn, the gardens feature great displays of azaleas and rhododendrons, daffodils and bluebells, and glowing trees such as the maple. It was in the house (not NT) that Edward Gibbon wrote his famous *Decline and Fall of the Roman Empire*, and he is buried in the Sheffield family vault in Fletching church, just opposite the eastern gateway of the estate.

Garden open 11 a.m.-6 p.m. Tuesday to Saturday, 2 p.m.-6 p.m. or sunset Sundays and Bank Holidays, April to mid-November; but closed Good Friday and Tuesday after Bank Holiday.

House open 2 p.m.-5 p.m. Easter Sunday and Monday, then Wednesdays, Thursdays, Sundays and Bank Holidays in May, June, September and October. Fee. Shop. Refreshments for pre-booked parties only. WC.

9 CHAILEY COMMON

Take southbound A22. At Wych Cross fork right on A275 towards Lewes. A mile south of Sheffield Park station is a right turn signposted Warrs Hill Road Hospital, leading to a large car-park marked by a board for Chailey Common Nature Reserve. There are walks across the rough common towards Chailey Heritage, dominated by the remains of a post mill. Other informal parking spaces can be found in the bushes to either side of A275 just south of its dog-leg crossing of A272.

10 PILTDOWN PICNIC SITE

Follow directions as for preceding entry, but instead of crossing
A275 on Chailey Common turn left on it towards Uckfield. Just
past the inn with a sign showing the skull of the Piltdown Man –
supposedly the remains of a prehistoric 'missing link' excavated
from gravel diggings on Pilt Down, but proved in 1953-4 to have
been an archaeological hoax – turn right on minor road signposted
Shortbridge. Between the golf course and a wide lake is a
rough-and-ready picnic site, with a pleasant stroll round the banks.

NEARBY FEATURES:

About three miles south down the same minor road is Isfield,
where enthusiastic restoration has worked wonders on the bright
little village station, yet another victim of branch-line closures. It
is hoped over the years to develop a section of track as 'The
Lavender Line' and run steam services.

Beeches Farm, Buckham Hill, about halfway between Piltdown
and Isfield on the above-mentioned road. A sixteenth-century
farmhouse (the house not open to the public) with extensive
gardens including a sunken garden, trees and wide views over the
Sussex countryside. Gardens open 10 a.m.-5 p.m. daily all year
round. Very small fee.

11 WAKEHURST PLACE GARDEN (NT), near Ardingly

Take southbound A22. At Newchapel turn right on westbound
B2028 and south through Turners Hill. A mile and a half north of
Ardingly are the entrance and large car-park for Wakehurst Place to
the right of the road. There is an admission fee (children under
sixteen less than half-price), but the variety and extent of the
gardens and open spaces within more than justify this.

The house and grounds are leased by the National Trust to the
administrators of the Royal Botanic Garden at Kew, and here, as at
Bedgebury Pinetum (see earlier entry), trees and shrubs for research
purposes have been admirably integrated with heath and cottage
gardens. A number of distinctive features, including Southern
Hemisphere plants with an emphasis on New Zealand natives,
derive from the personal interests of Gerald Loder, Lord Wakehurst,
during the first three decades of this century. A sequence of lakes

developed from old hammer-ponds of the local iron industry form a water garden. Avenues radiating from the mansion, including a rhododendron walk, provide beautifully calculated vistas and a network of little interlinking paths.

There are rock terraces in the main gardens themselves, but most appealing to children are the misshapen, overhanging rocks of the remoter walks through Westwood Valley and Bloomers Valley (so called not because of its floral blooms but because of the bloomeries or early furnaces which once operated here), where massive roots of ancient yews twist over sandstone outcrops like the writhings of octopus tentacles. From the part known as Loder Valley can be seen the waters of Ardingly Reservoir.

In Ardingly church is a memorial brass to a fifteenth-century Wakehurst heiress who, with her sister, was abducted by the brothers of their guardian, Sir John Culpeper of Bedgebury. Later there were two apparently happy marriages: one couple produced no children, but Nicholas and Elizabeth had ten sons and eight daughters, all shown huddled together on the brass.

Gardens open daily 10 a.m.-7 p.m. April to September, 10 a.m. to dusk the rest of the year. Closed Christmas Day and New Year's Day. Fee. Refreshments in the mansion April to October. Shop. WC.

Alternative approach: a visit to Wakehurst Place can be incorporated with explorations of Ashdown Forest (see earlier entry). At junction of A275 and A272 south of Sheffield Park, turn right on westbound A272 towards Haywards Heath, then right on northbound B2028 through Lindfield to Wakehurst Place.

NEARBY FEATURE:

Borde Hill Garden. A private garden about two miles south of Balcombe, on right of minor road towards Haywards Heath. Parking and picnic site. Woodland walks, extensive gardens and parkland around manor house, with rare trees and shrubs, azaleas and magnolias. Open Saturday and Sunday 10 a.m.-6 p.m. March and October, plus Wednesday, Thursday and Bank Holidays April to September. Fee. Refreshments. Plant shop. WC.

FROM JUNCTION

7

12 ST LEONARDS FOREST, near Horsham

Take southbound M23 towards Brighton. Join A23 south of
Crawley. Eastbound minor road from Pease Pottage runs through
Tilgate Forest, once supposedly the haunt of a dragon and still
mysterious, with little to offer in the way of formal parking and
picnic sites, but footpaths leading into its depths. The westbound
road towards Horsham has informal roadside parking, and little
woodland roads linking the hamlets of Faygate, Colgate and other
secretive little clusters.

NEARBY FEATURE:

Leonardslee Gardens, Lower Beeding. Can be reached through St
Leonards Forest via Ashfold and Lower Beeding; or, starting as
above, continue on southbound A23 to Handcross, then take
westbound A279 to Lower Beeding. The gardens are at the
southern junction of A279 and A281. A spring garden celebrated
for its rhododendrons and azaleas, around a valley shimmering
with a long lake incorporating an old furnace pond. Open 10
a.m.-6 p.m. daily, late April to early June; also 10 a.m.-5 p.m.
October weekends. Fee. Refreshments. WC.

13 DITCHLING COMMON COUNTRY PARK, near Burgess Hill

On a crowded Bank Holiday weekend, traffic might be so congested
as to put this beyond our time limit, but in normal conditions it
should be attainable without too much stress.

Take southbound M23 towards Brighton and join A23 south of
Crawley. At Handcross turn off through village on B2114 to
Haywards Heath. Turn south on B2112 towards Ditchling. At
crossroads on heath, signposted to Burgess Hill on the right, turn

left to car-park and picnic site on rough commonland. There are unhindered walks all over the heath and down into the captivating village of Ditchling itself.

Ditchling Beacon may, similarly, under certain conditions lie just beyond our chosen limit, but if one has got this far it is a pity not to pursue the route for another couple of miles. The B2112 continues south through Ditchling village and up a steep, winding slope of the South Downs to a parking place high on the summit, commanding views over the Downs and the Weald below. Here there was once literally a beacon, one of a chain kindled in the time of Queen Elizabeth I when the Spanish Armada hove into view. The long-distance footpath of the South Downs Way cuts directly across the site.

Alternative approaches: (a) from Ashdown Forest (see earlier entries) continue on southbound A275, turn right on westbound minor road towards Burgess Hill, and the above-mentioned parking and picnic site will now be found on the right; (b) from M25 junction 8 follow southbound A217 through Reigate and then southbound A23 to Handcross, and proceed as in original directions.

NEARBY FEATURE:

Nymans Garden (NT). From the turn-off through Handcross village, the entrance to the garden is on the left of B2114, clearly signposted. Hydrangeas, magnolias, roses and rhododendrons abound in these trim formal gardens, set about a house whose southern façade is a creeper-grown, romantic ruin after a fire many years ago. There is a horseshoe-shaped pinetum, a laurel walk to a sunken garden and a wistaria-laden pergola; woodland walks offer now and then a glimpse of Chanctonbury Ring on the South Downs.

Open 11 a.m.-7 p.m. or sunset daily from April to October, except Monday and Friday – but open Bank Holiday Mondays. Fee. Refreshments in tea-house by car-park. WC.

14 WOODS MILL, near Henfield

Take southbound M23 and A23 towards Brighton. At Albourne turn right on westbound B2116. There is a picnic site at the junction of B2116 and A281. Turn left on southbound A281 through Henfield on to A2031. Woods Mill is on the left of the road a mile south, at junction with Horn Lane.

The eighteenth-century watermill is the headquarters of the Sussex Trust for Nature Conservation, situated in a natural environment rich in birds and insects. It has a turning millwheel and houses a wildlife and countryside exhibition, including live animals and insects, an aquarium, an observation beehive and audio-visual programmes. A twenty-five-foot-high model of an oak tree is set in the well of the staircase, from which it can be studied at every level from roots to leaves. A nature trail runs through the woodland and marsh of a fifteen-acre nature reserve, with a lake and streams. Nets are provided for children to catch and identify specimens from a dipping pond.

Open 2 p.m.-6 p.m. Tuesday, Wednesday, Thursday and Saturday, and 11 a.m.-6 p.m. Sundays and Bank Holidays, from Easter to late September. Car-park free. Admission fee to exhibition and nature trail (reduced rate for children under sixteen). Shop. WC.

FROM JUNCTION

8

15 CHIPHOUSE WOOD, Chipstead

Take northbound A217 to Kingswood. At roundabout in Kingswood turn right on westbound B2032 towards railway station, and at T-junction turn right to follow B2032 over railway bridge. Immediately over bridge, turn sharp left along minor road to entrance to wood. There are twenty acres in all – eight of formerly ploughed land, and twelve of oak woodland. The Woodland Trust is carrying out a careful programme of afforesting the open land in order to link up patches of existing woodland, while at the same time preserving grassy glades and rides for the benefit of wildlife and for visitors. There are several footpaths for the use of appreciative walkers.

16 BANSTEAD COMMONS and BANSTEAD WOOD

Take northbound A217 to Kingswood. At roundabout in Kingswood turn left on westbound B2032 for Walton on the Hill, or right on eastbound B2032 for Banstead Wood.

Banstead Commons in fact begin at Walton, with walks and cycle tracks wandering off from Withybed Corner. No parking is allowed on the paths, so cars have to be left in the village or on roadside lay-bys. Epsom Races began on Walton Downs, but the only horses to be seen nowadays are on the bridlepaths, and modern building has encroached on much of the once open land.

To reach further large expanses of green common, return along the eastbound B3032 to Kingswood, and at the T-junction near the railway station turn right to follow B3032 over the railway bridge. Approaching Banstead, turn left up B2219, Lower Park Road. There is a large car-park on the left, on the edge of wide tracts of undulating grassland and Banstead Wood. On the other side of Lower Park Road is an ascent to another seventy-five acres of open space on Park Downs. WC.

17 HORTON COUNTRY PARK, near Ewell

Take northbound A217 to Burgh Heath, and A240 to Ewell. The country park, about a mile west of Ewell West railway station, encompasses about 240 acres of wood and grassland.

18 REIGATE HILL

Take southbound A217 towards Reigate, then immediately right into Wray Lane. The car park has a refreshment kiosk and WC. From it a path is carried by footbridge across the main road. To both sides of the A217 are the slopes, glades and footpaths of Wingate Hill (or Reigate Hill) and Gatton Park, crossed by the long-distance path of the North Downs Way.

Sheltering within a clump of chestnut trees near Gatton church are the classical columns and roof of an incongruous relic looking like a Greek temple. Actually it served in the eighteenth century as a town hall, built by the then lord of the manor so that election results – in those days a foregone conclusion in such a 'pocket' or 'rotten' borough – could be announced with due ceremony.

Another folly, this time a circular edifice with a ring of columns, stands on Colley Hill and provides welcome shelter during any sudden shower. Expanses of crisp, short grass both on Colley Hill and on Reigate Hill offer ample space for picnics, as well as views of neighbouring hills and, across the roofs of the town, the Weald.

FROM JUNCTION

9

19 ASHTEAD and EPSOM COMMONS

Take northbound A243 towards Kingston-upon-Thames. To the left of the road past the golf course are Telegraph Hill and the footpaths of Stoke Wood. Ashtead Common, with pathways weaving between solid clusters of trees, lies to the right of the road, with access at several points, and overlaps with neighbouring Epsom Common.

NEARBY FEATURE:
Chessington Zoo. Beside A243. More than sixty acres of zoological gardens with birds and animals, including chimpanzees and gorillas. Children's zoo. During the summer a funfair, free circus and narrow-gauge railway. Fee. Refreshments. Picnic area. Open 11 a.m.-4 p.m. November to March, 10 a.m.-5 p.m. April to October. Closed Christmas Day. WC.

20 OXSHOTT and ESHER COMMONS

Take northbound A244 through Oxshott towards Esher. On Oxshott Heath there are parking spaces to the left of the road, one near Oxshott station railway bridge. Continuing northwards across the A3, there is a car-park to the left immediately beyond the roundabout.

The Black Pond in the south-east corner of Esher Common provides an informal swimming-pool, with changing-sheds under the trees.

Keen walkers can cross A244 and pursue footpaths through the trees of Arbrook Common.

NEARBY FEATURE:
Claremont Landscape Garden (NT). Beside A307 just south of Esher. Some fifty acres of one of the earliest landscaped gardens in England, begun by Vanbrugh and later extended by 'Capability' Brown. Clive of India bought the property and pulled down the original house to make way for the present one. The house is now a school for the children of Christian Scientists, open to visitors (fee) 2 p.m.-6 p.m. first weekend in each month from February to November.

After years of neglect the gardens have been faithfully restored to their original appearance, including a lake, an island with a pavilion, turf amphitheatre, grotto and avenues with finely contrived viewpoints. Open 9 a.m.-7 p.m. or sunset daily, April to October; 9 a.m.-4 p.m. daily, November to March, except Christmas Day and New Year's Day. Small fee. Refreshments at lakeside kiosk (closed November to end of February). WC.

21 WALTON-ON-THAMES and SHEPPERTON
Take northbound A244 through Esher to Walton-on-Thames. On the north-west bank of the river by Walton bridge are a large marina and extensive grassy spaces along the river edge. Immediately beyond that the road through Shepperton towards Chertsey passes a large car-park to the left, serving wide grassy spaces in a pleasant surround of trees, leading back down towards the river.

22 BOX HILL, near Dorking
Leave on southbound A24 towards Dorking. At Burford Bridge roundabout just north of Dorking turn sharp left on minor road signposted Box Hill. There is a large parking and picnic site, with refreshments and WC, immediately to the left of the road. The North Downs Way and Pilgrims' Way run close to it, crossing the modern A24 by modern means — a pedestrian subway — and leading on to stepping-stones across the River Mole at the foot of the hill.

A short distance uphill, an unsignposted right turn leads to a twisting, steeply climbing road to the summit, with ample parking and picnic spaces, information centre and restaurant. WC.

Box Hill takes its name from the box trees which cling to its soaring sides. In winter tobogganers and even a few skiers make use of the barer northern slopes. At all times of year it is ideal terrain for walking, scrambling up between the trees and stopping to make the most of viewpoints over the wide panorama of the world below. Waymarked walks from the information centre include one comparatively short walk which provides a sort of visual summary of the area's main features, and one longer nature trail explains the natural history of the region in more detail.

Just below the summit a stone 'pulpit' faces out over the Surrey Weald, with magnificent views to the South Downs, taking in the unmistakeable clump of Chanctonbury Ring in Sussex. Carved into the parapet are markers identifying this and other distant landmarks. The monument commemorates Leopold Salomons of Norbury Park, who donated 230 acres of this down and woodland to the nation in 1914, since expanded to more than nine hundred acres.

Another eminent local character was Major Labelliere of Dorking, whose grave is marked by a stone near the top. He believed that the world was all the wrong way up in his time, and insisted on being buried upside down so that when resurrected in better times he would prove to be right way up.

23 HEADLEY HEATH, near Leatherhead

From Box Hill (see directions for preceding entry) there is a delightful drive along the heights, swinging round north through what is known as Little Switzerland to the expanses of Mickleham Downs – stopping to explore Headley Heath on foot. The road along the ridge descends to a junction with B2033. Turn left on this towards Leatherhead. There are two large car-parks to the left of the road, from which one can walk over great tracts of gorse and bracken, with clumps of shimmering birch trees and chalky little hollows.

Alternative approach: B2033 through Headley is signposted from Leatherhead, so that one can follow the above route in reverse.

24 BOOKHAM and BANKS COMMONS, Great Bookham

Leave on southbound A24 towards Dorking. South of Leatherhead turn right on westbound A246 to Great Bookham. Turn right into the village, past the church, to car-park at commonside near the railway station. There are two other parking sites on other fringes of the commons, each leading on to numerous walks, and a number of roadside lay-bys.

The 450 acres consist of open spaces which were once grazing clearings in the rich woodland of oak and holly, with plenty of blackberries in season. There are also a number of old fishponds. As a Site of Special Scientific Interest the area has been continuously documented since 1940 by the London Natural History Society, and five hundred species of flowering plants have been identified as well as ferns, mosses and fungi.

NEARBY FEATURE:

Polesden Lacey (NT). Well signposted from A246 through Great Bookham. The Regency house was once the dramatist Sheridan's home and later that of a wealthy Edwardian hostess. The Duke and Duchess of York, later to become King George VI and Queen Elizabeth, spent part of their honeymoon here. There are exhibits of furniture, tapestries, silver, and Edwardian photograph albums. House open 2 p.m.-5 p.m. or sunset Saturday and Sunday, March and November; 2 p.m.-6 p.m. Saturday, Sunday, Tuesday, Wednesday, Thursday and Bank Holiday Monday (but closed Tuesday after Bank Holiday), April to October. Fee. Refreshments. WC.

Extensive gardens (fee) open daily all year round, 11 a.m.-sunset.

25 RANMORE COMMON, near Dorking

Take southbound A24 towards Dorking. Turn right on minor road towards West Humble and Great Bookham, past Box Hill railway station, and left onto Ranmore Common. At intervals over this long stretch of rough grassy land on the North Downs scarp, with woods rising gently to the north, there are several car-parks with picnic tables and benches, and plenty of room for informal parking on the open Common.

The North Downs Way and Pilgrims' Way cross the Common on the way down to Burford Bridge and the stepping-stones across the River Mole.

Alternative approach: follow directions as for Great Bookham and Polesden Lacey (preceding entry), then pass Polesden Lacey by minor road towards West Humble, and turn right on minor road across Ranmore Common.

26 ABINGER COMMON, near Dorking

Take southbound A24 to outskirts of Dorking. Follow signposted route round the outskirts to avoid the town centre and join westbound A25 towards Guildford.

Just beyond Wotton is a left turn onto a minor road signposted Abinger Common. On the left of this road, sunk between deep banks and trees – easily missed by anyone driving too fast – is another minor road signposted Friday Street, leading in a short distance to a similarly concealed car-park serving a County Council Open Space. There are woodland walks and quiet, shaded clearings between the trees. An odd little sheltered site near the B2126 from Abinger Hammer to Forest Green is in fact the remains of a mesolithic pit dwelling excavated in the 1950s. The common runs on to Abinger Forest and to Holmwood Common on both sides of the A24 south of Dorking.

27 HOLMBURY HILL, near Dorking

Follow directions as for preceding entry, but continue along westbound A25 to Abinger Hammer and turn left on southbound B2126, also signposted Abinger Common. There is car-parking space by the youth hostel in Holmbury St Mary. The sandy slopes of Holmbury Hill, clad in bracken and pine trees, climb to the ramparts of an Iron Age hill fort whose triple banks, though damaged by sand and gravel digging, can still be identified. From a memorial stone seat thoughtfully installed for those out of breath after the climb there are far-ranging views over the Weald, and eastward towards Leith Hill.

NEARBY FEATURE:

Minor roads on the eastern side of Dorking, and others crossing A24 from Holmwood and Holmbury lead to Brockham. In Brockham's derelict quarry is a museum of old quarry engines, with a short stretch of narrow-gauge track. This was the setting for scenes from a *Dr Who* television serial a few years ago. There is an agreeable riverside walk from Brockham to Betchworth.

28 LEITH HILL, near Dorking

Follow directions as for Abinger Common but, instead of turning towards Friday Street and car-park, continue on minor road which begins to climb Leith Hill. Alternative approach: in Abinger Hammer take southbound B2126 as for Abinger Common and Holmbury Hill, and beyond Holmbury St Mary take minor road to left up Leith Hill. There is a large car-park below the summit, with woodland glades for picnics and a long but not too steep walk up to the breezy open space around Leith Hill tower.

At 965 feet the summit is the highest point in south-east England, and the top of the tower continues to over twelve hundred feet. It was built in 1766 by Richard Hull, owner of neighbouring Leith Hill Place – later the home of the composer Ralph Vaughan Williams. This house is not open to the public, but they are permitted free into the woodlands with displays of azaleas and rhododendrons.

Legend has it that Richard Hull had himself buried under his tower, instructing his executors that he must be interred upside down since, like a similar eccentric on Box Hill (see earlier entry), he had calculated that by Judgement Day the world would have turned completely on its axis and he was determined to come face to face with his Maker the right way up.

A shorter but steeper and more energetic way of reaching the tower is from a minor road swinging round the slope towards Coldharbour. From a rough car-park on the left begins a steep, slippery path with sections of steep flights of steps and the occasional handrail.

On the eastern side of the hill is prehistoric Anstiebury Camp, with triple earthen ramparts, planted over with trees in the eighteenth century. The line of the Roman Stane Street from

Chichester to London skirts the site only half a mile away. In a later century, Leith Hill was the setting for a savage battle between Danish invaders who, after ravaging London and Canterbury, camped at Anstiebury on their way to Winchester. Here they were defeated by Ethelwulf, father of Alfred the Great. Bones found in a nearby field in 1882 suggest that it may have been the burial ground of those killed in the struggle.

29 PRESTIGE WOOD, Hammond's Copse, Newdigate

Take southbound A24 through Dorking, and shortly after Holmwood station turn left on eastbound minor road to Newdigate, then north-east through Parkgate. Hammond's Copse lies to the right of the road about half a mile out of the village.

Its continuing existence is largely due to the efforts of the Woodland Trust, who learned of the owner's intention of selling off the wood, most probably in due course to be cleared for agriculture, and with the aid of Prestige Hotels – whose name has now been bestowed on this section of Hammond's Copse – took it over. Although parts have been cleared and replanted in recent times, a considerable section is ancient woodland, a great deal of it hazel coppice under oak trees.

30 GLOVER'S WOOD, Charlwood

Take southbound A24 through Dorking and eastbound minor road through Newdigate and Parkgate as in preceding entry. Continue towards Charlwood and then take minor road to the south-west. Glover's Wood lies to the right of the road. Its best access is by footpath leading westward from Charlwood.

Here again, as in the preceding site, the Woodland Trust have been at work, preserving the character of the ancient wood and its more recent developments. There are some interesting features, including a sphagnum bog, and wych elm and small-leaved lime – rare in this part of the country.

Although bombarded by the thunderings of Gatwick airport, less than two miles away, the shaded footpaths offer the visitor a welcome to woodland which manages to remain surprisingly remote and soothing.

NEARBY FEATURE:
Gatwick Zoo and Aviaries, Charlwood. See entry for Outwood
Common earlier in this chapter.

FROM JUNCTION

10

31 OCKHAM and WISLEY COMMONS

This area spills over into the south-western division dealt with in
Chapter 4 but it is sensible to deal with it here, all in one piece.

Take A3 south-west towards Guildford. Ockham Common lies
to the left of the road, Wisley to the right.

Ockham is heavily wooded, with a virtual forest of closely packed
rhododendrons. Peeping above the trees of Chatley Heath in the
eastern quarter of the area is a tower on Telegraph Hill, one of a
chain of thirteen erected during the Napoleonic Wars to relay
semaphore messages between Portsmouth and the Admiralty in
London. Today it looks mutely down on a most agreeable open
space for picnics. In the south-west corner between the A3 and a
minor road across the Common is Bolder Mere, a wide patch of lake
which is shallow enough to freeze easily, and so provides
opportunities for skating in hard winters.

Wisley Common is more open and criss-crossed with footpaths.

NEARBY FEATURE:
Royal Horticultural Society Garden, Wisley, signposted off A3.
Extensive ornamental and specialist gardens, lawns, plantations
and fruit and vegetable plots. Advisory service, plant centre and
shop. Picnic area and licensed restaurant. WC.

Free car-park, but fee for admission to gardens; children
half-price, children under six free. Open 10 a.m.-7 p.m. or dusk,
Monday to Saturday all year round except Christmas Day;
Sundays 2 p.m.-7 p.m. or dusk.

32 BUSHY PARK, near Kingston-upon-Thames

Take eastbound M3. At M3 junction 1 take A308 towards
Hampton. Between Hampton and Kingston bridge, Bushy Park lies
to the north of the road, Hampton Court Park to the south –
generous expanses of parkland surrounded by the fashionable
housing estates and older lanes of Richmond, Hampton,
Teddington and Twickenham. Bushy Park is bisected by the
straight line of Chestnut Avenue, broken only by two graceful arcs
framing the Diana Fountain. This drive was intended by
Christopher Wren as a sumptuous grand avenue worthy of the
approach to Hampton Court Palace and its surrounding parkland.
Somehow the various aspects were never quite integrated, but what
remains is beautifully proportioned and rewarding: there are walks,
plantations, ponds, the amiably meandering 'Longford River' and
acres of free open space. Across the road Hampton Court Park, too,
is open free to the public until dusk.

Alternative approaches: (a) from M25 junction 10 take
eastbound A3 to Esher, then northbound A309 over Hampton
Court Bridge; (b) from M25 junction 13 take eastbound A308 to
Hampton Court and Bushy Park.

NEARBY FEATURE:

Hampton Court Palace. Set close to the entrance to Hampton
Court Park, the palace was the grandiose creation of Cardinal
Wolsey, later offered as a placatory gift to King Henry VIII.
Three of Henry's honeymoons were spent there, as was Charles
I's honeymoon. Charles's great antagonist Oliver Cromwell also
loved the place, and his daughter was married here in the Chapel
Royal. State rooms rich in royal associations are open to the
public daily all year round, with restricted Sunday afternoon
hours October to March. Fee. WC.

Wren's alterations in the late seventeenth and early eighteenth centuries included the commissioning of the great French ironsmith Jean Tijou to construct the superb wrought-iron gates. There is a fascinating maze in the grounds, and a grapevine planted in 1768 has proliferated so magnificently that it seems to promise, one fine season, a connoisseurs' vintage of Château Hampton.

FROM JUNCTION

13

33 RICHMOND PARK

Take eastbound A308 through Bushy Park and Hampton Court Park (as in preceding entry) and over Kingston bridge. Turn north-east on A308 to join A3 Kingston bypass near the Robin Hood Gate into Richmond Park.

Alternative approaches to this entrance: (a) from M25 junction 9 take northbound A243, then north-east on A3 to junction near Robin Hood Gate; (b) from M25 junction 10 take A3 north-east to junction near Robin Hood Gate.

There are five other main 'carriage gates' as well as entrances for pedestrians, which can of course be reached from other preferred approaches. Open daily during daylight hours, each has a large car-park immediately inside, and there are other parking spaces within the park. One at Broomfield Hill has a neighbouring refreshment kiosk; one specially installed for the Isabella Plantation is only a few minutes' stroll from that charming little woodland garden, hidden away in a dell with rivulets, azaleas and rhododendrons, seen at its best in late May and early autumn.

The grounds of this royal domain, the largest enclosed park in Britain, include two golf courses, a polo ground and several football pitches. Model boats may be sailed on Adam's Pond near the Sheen Gate, and there are other ponds at various points. Pen Ponds, first known as the Canals when they were dug in the middle of the eighteenth century, are available for skating when the ice has been pronounced safe enough by the keepers. One of them changed its name yet again, in due course, to Leg of Mutton Pond, by which it is best known today.

Kite-flying is a great pastime on the more exposed slopes. Picnicking is allowed anywhere, but the public are forbidden to feed the deer, friendly as they may be. Even simply driving round the main outer road is a pleasure, with its glimpses of herds of red and fallow deer and, every now and then challenging the treetops, the distant forest of London skyscrapers or the tower blocks of flats above Roehampton. But it is above all a place for getting out of the car and walking, under old oaks or through the bracken, around ponds and along well-trodden paths and rides.

Neighbouring the northern fringe of the park is East Sheen Common, fifty acres of open space given to the National Trust in 1908 and now managed by the borough of Richmond. On the other side of Roehampton Vale main road (A3) is Wimbledon Common, rougher and less disciplined than Richmond Park but spacious and ideal for walking and picnicking.

NEARBY FEATURES:

Kew Bridge Engines and Water Supply Museum, in Green Dragon Lane, Kew Bridge Road, Brentford. A pumping station with museum displays of London water supply history, workshop, forges, and any number of beam engines, several of them working. Open 11 a.m.-5 p.m. every weekend and Bank Holiday except Christmas. Fee. Refreshments. WC.

Royal Botanic Gardens, Kew. About three hundred acres displaying more than fifty thousand varieties of flowers and plants. Glasshouses, a towering pagoda, Kew Palace and the cottage retreat of Queen Charlotte, wife of King George III. Gardens open 10 a.m. to between 4 p.m. and 8 p.m. according to season. Closed Christmas Day and New Year's Day. Small fee. Refreshments. Shop. WC.

Separate small fees for the palace and cottage, open April to September (cottage Saturday, Sunday and Bank Holidays only).

34 HAM COMMON

Take eastbound A308 to Kingston, and over the bridge turn left on northbound A307 towards Richmond. At crossroads with B352, Ham Common is on the right. A short minor road signposted to Ham House leads down to a free car-park on the edge of the Thames. There is a broad riverside walk with delightful trees, wild flowers and grasses towards Twickenham in one direction, and in the other across the expanses of Petersham Meadows to the slopes of Richmond Hill with its commanding view of the curving river. On the far bank of the river is a vista of Marble Hill Park (see below).

Alternative approach: after crossing Richmond Park from Robin Hood Gate (see preceding entry) leave by Ham Gate onto Ham Common.

NEARBY FEATURE:

Ham House (NT). A graceful seventeenth-century house now used as an offshoot of the Victoria & Albert Museum in South Kensington, housing furniture from Charles II's time. The seventeenth-century garden has been restored in recent times.

House open daily except Monday (but open most Bank Holiday Mondays) 2 p.m.-6 p.m. April to the end of September, noon-4 p.m. October to the end of March. Fee. Refreshments in garden restaurant. WC.

Garden open during above times, free.

35 MARBLE HILL PARK, Twickenham

Take eastbound A308. At junction with M3 take A316 and A305 north-east through Twickenham. Marble Hill Park and Orleans Park lie to the right, between the road and the river. WC.

Marble Hill is a fine open space of richly green grass fringed and dotted with clumps of well-tended trees. There is a children's enclosed playground near the river, and huge plane trees shelter the beginnings of a riverside path to Richmond.

Marble Hill House, built in the early eighteenth century for King George II's mistress Henrietta Howard, is a notable example of English Palladian architecture, with a collection of Georgian furniture and paintings. Open 10 a.m.-5 p.m. (4 p.m. November to January) daily except Fridays and 24 and 25 December. Free entry. Refreshments April to September.

Beside the park is the more secretive walled woodland, somewhat unkempt but very inviting, of Orleans Park, carpeted with daffodils in springtime. An eighteenth-century house which once stood here became the home of Louis Philippe, Duc d'Orléans, during much of his exile here before returning to France as king. In 1927 the building was demolished save for a baroque octagon beside which, today, is an art gallery featuring temporary exhibitions. Open every afternoon except for Mondays (but open Bank Holiday Mondays) and Christmas. Free of charge.

36 OSTERLEY PARK

Take A308 to Staines, then A30 north-west to junction with A4 in Hounslow. Follow eastbound A4 towards London. Just past Osterley underground station turn left on Thornbury Road, leading straight to car-park within Osterley Park.

The 150 acres of landscaped gardens and parkland are open free daily, 10 a.m.-8 p.m. or sunset if earlier, with lakes, a garden house and a Doric temple where past owners enjoyed taking their meals in sylvan surroundings.

Osterley Park House (NT) is used by the Victoria & Albert Museum of South Kensington as one of their branch collections. Originally an Elizabethan mansion, it was adapted in the eighteenth century into a neo-Classical villa, with an imposing double portico, though still retaining the original Tudor stable block. The museum authorities have restored the sumptuous state rooms, including a drawing-room with a dizzyingly ornate ceiling, and a charming tapestry room. The National Trust and the Royal Parks division of the Department of the Environment co-operate on maintaining the grounds.

House open daily except Monday (but open Bank Holiday Mondays), 2 p.m.-5 p.m. April to September, noon-4 p.m. October to March, except May Day, Good Friday, Christmas Eve, Christmas Day, Boxing Day and New Year's Day. Fee. Refreshments April to September. WC.

Alternative approach: from M25 junction 15 take eastbound M4. At M4 junction 3 turn south to A4 roundabout and take eastbound A4 as above.

4 SOUTH-WEST

JUNCTIONS
9-11

Most of the sites dealt with in this chapter are perhaps more comfortably accessible from junction 10 than from the others; but drivers living closer to junctions 9 or 11 will probably prefer to use those and link up with alternative routes where most convenient. Various suggestions along these lines are made in individual entries, without claiming to cover every eventuality. Similarly, there is an unavoidable overlap between the south and south-western divisions of the book.

The characteristics of the countryside here are themselves overlapping and interwoven. The sandy moorlands of Surrey have such an acid soil that they have never been of much value to farmers, so that wild wastes of heath and rough woodland remain – save for tracts taken over by the military – for the benefit of walkers and picnickers. One common runs into another, or the boundaries are blurred by scrub and trees, so that from a car-park or lay-by serving one site it is easy to wander on to another. Here there are fewer restrictions, far more freedom, for strollers or energetic walkers than in almost any other part of south-east England, and it is hardly necessary to be too specific about starting- or finishing-points. Quite apart from marked car-parks, there are innumerable informal roadside pull-ins and sheltered glades. Although a fair number of the little towns and villages can justifiably be classed as commuters' dormitories, the traffic of their roads is rarely fierce enough to disturb the age-old mysteries of hill, heath, and wood.

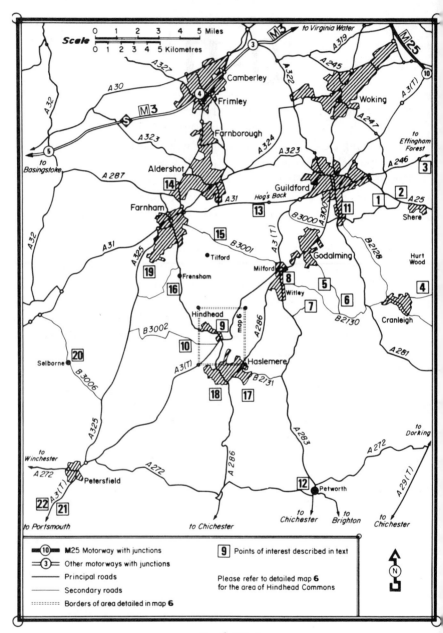

South-West

KEY

1   Newlands Corner, near Guildford
2   The Silent Pool, near Shere
3   The Sheepleas, Effingham Forest
4   Hurtwood and Pitch Hill, near Ewhurst
5   Winkworth Arboretum, near Godalming
6   Hascombe Hill, near Godalming
7   Hascombe-Hambledon Woods, near Godalming
8   Witley and Milford Commons
9   Hindhead Commons
10   Ludshott Common and Waggoners Wells, near Hindhead
11   Wey and Godalming Navigation
12   Petworth Park
13   Hog's Back Picnic Site
14   Rowhill Nature Reserve, near Farnham
15   Crooksbury Hill, Tilford
16   Frensham Ponds and Country Park
17   Black Down, near Haslemere
18   Marley Common, near Haslemere
19   Alice Holt Forest, near Farnham
20   Selborne Common
21   Queen Elizabeth Country Park, near Petersfield
22   Butser Ancient Farm, near Petersfield

FROM JUNCTION 9

1 NEWLANDS CORNER, near Guildford

Take westbound A246 towards Guildford. At West Clandon crossroads turn left to join A25 south and east towards Dorking. At Newlands Corner, nearly six hundred feet up on Albury Downs, is a huge car-park with refreshment kiosk and WC. It commands views over the Weald below to the South Downs. The Pilgrims' Way ascends the slopes below, and other footpaths wind their way down to meet it.

Overlooking the village of Chilworth is St Martha's Chapel, one of the stopping-places for rest and prayer along the pilgrims' route. Paths, tracks and a narrow road converge on Albury village and Albury Park, whose gardens, laid out by the diarist John Evelyn, are frequently open to the public.

Alternative approach: from M25 junction 10 take A3 south-west towards Guildford. A short way beyond Ripley turn left on southbound A247 past Clandon Park and cross A246 to pick up A25 and proceed as above.

NEARBY FEATURES:

Clandon Park (NT). Beside A247 through West Clandon. An early-eighteenth-century house in Palladian style with a soaring, two-storeyed marble entrance hall. Pictures, furniture, a military museum and a collection of Chinese porcelain birds. Fascinating old kitchen. Picnic area near car-park. Fee. Refreshments. WC.

Open 2 p.m.-6 p.m. daily except Monday and Friday, April to mid-October; but open Bank Holiday Mondays, closed Tuesday after a Bank Holiday, and closed Good Friday. Garden Centre in grounds open daily all year round.

Hatchlands (NT). Beside A246 east of East Clandon. An eighteenth-century brick house built for Admiral Boscawen, with interiors by Robert Adam. A Boscawen exhibition room, parkland, gardens. Fee. Refreshments in old kitchen. WC.

Open 2 p.m.-6 p.m. Wednesday, Thursday and Sunday from April to late October.

2 THE SILENT POOL, near Shere

Take either route recommended in preceding entry, and then continue on eastbound A25 towards Dorking. Just over a mile along this road, to the left of a dual carriageway section, is parking for the Silent Pool. (Note that if approached from the westbound A25 this can be reached through a signposted gap in the central reservation of the dual carriageway.)

This is a secluded, pretty little spot in the heart of a wood, with a path winding round the banks of a still, dark pool which, even with modern traffic rushing past so close, preserves an uncanny silence and eeriness. Legend has it that the daughter of a local woodman was bathing in what was then known as Sherborne Pond when King John appeared on the bank and laughingly drove his horse into the water after her. Terrified, she blundered into the deepest part of the pool. Hearing her screams, her brother dashed to the rescue and flung himself into the water. But neither of them could swim: they sank to the bottom, locked in each other's arms, and drowned.

NEARBY FEATURE:

Shalford Mill. Although this is not a familiar tourist attraction open to all comers, it is a pity to be in the neighbourhood and not take an appreciative glance at it. Across the road from the Silent Pool, the A248 through Albury towards a junction with A281 a mile and a half south of Guildford offers a view of this picturesque eighteenth-century mill straddling the little River Tillingbourne. Associated with it is a more modern legend than that of the girl drowned in the pool. An anonymous group of idealists anxious to do their bit towards rural preservation gave themselves the name of 'Ferguson's Gang' and from the 1930s onwards made substantial donations to the National Trust as well as repairing Shalford Mill and using it as headquarters for their secret meetings. Those with a genuine interest in the building can obtain the key during daylight hours from 45 The Street, Shalford.

3 THE SHEEPLEAS, Effingham Forest

Take westbound A246 through Great Bookham. Halfway between East Horsley and West Horsley is a car-park beside St Mary's

Church, from which a footpath leads into the Sheepleas. Here is an arboretum with a variety of plantations, including some splendid beeches, and Mountain Wood forest walk through woods and glades.

Other footpaths criss-cross Effingham Forest, Netley Heath and Hackhurst Downs, some areas cared for by the county as designated open spaces, some by the National Trust.

Alternative approaches: (a) as above, but in East Horsley turn left on narrow minor road to secluded car-park under the trees on the right, serving the Sheepleas and Mountain Wood walk; (b) from M25 junction 10 take A3 southwest towards Guildford, turn left on southbound B2039 to East Horsley, and cross A246 onto minor road as in (a).

4 HURTWOOD and PITCH HILL, near Ewhurst

Take southbound A24 to Dorking. Follow signposted route round the outskirts to avoid the town centre and join westbound A25 towards Guildford. Turn left into Shere and take southbound minor road towards Ewhurst.

Hurstwood Common has dense patches of trees and any number of interweaving footpaths and glades suitable for picnics. At its southern tip, above Ewhurst village, the slopes climb up to the 843-foot summit of Pitch Hill, a climb well worth while for the incomparable views on every side, made all the richer by a well-planned clearance of trees from the summit itself.

Alternative approach: from M25 junction 10 take route to Silent Pool (see earlier entry), continue on eastbound A25, turn off to Shere village and follow directions as above. Also, a visit to this site could be tied in with that to Holmbury Hill in Chapter 3.

FROM JUNCTION

10

5 WINKWORTH ARBORETUM (NT), near Godalming

Take A3 south-west to Guildford, southbound A3100 to Godalming, and turn left on B2130 south-east towards Hascombe. On the left two miles from Godalming is a car-park for the arboretum. (There is another, smaller car-park on the far side of the grounds, reached by a minor road from the Guildford-Bramley A281.)

There is a small entrance fee, but this gives access to a beautiful hundred acres of wooded hillside with rare trees and shrubs, two lakes and fine views. Open all year round during daylight hours. Leaflets are available to guide one along trails at their best during the most colourful seasons – spring for bluebells and azaleas, autumn for the burnished hues of the leaves.

Refreshments in tea-room near car-park. Shop. WC.

6 HASCOMBE HILL, near Godalming

Follow directions as for Winkworth Arboretum in preceding entry, then continue into Hascombe village. Footpaths lead from here up Hascombe Hill, from whose greensand escarpment one can see over wooded vales to the Sussex Downs. Almost lost in the beech trees is an Iron Age promontory fort, thrusting out over a steep drop on the northern edge of the hill.

7 HASCOMBE-HAMBLEDON, near Godalming

The narrow winding roads and lanes of this withdrawn, tree-shaded region make explicit instructions regarding parking spaces and picnic sites difficult and, really, superfluous. One can enter this secluded little world either by branching off the suggested route for the two preceding entries or by taking the southbound A281 from Guildford and then turning right on westbound B2130.

Here is a region in which to drive slowly and choose one's own patch under the trees, one's own scramble up a slope or a footpath saunter in this delightful tangle of heath and woodland, hill and vale.

From Hambledon village a footpath leads to Hydon Heath and its highest point, Hydon Ball. These can also be reached from minor roads between Hascombe and Hydestile. There is a car-park under the trees at the foot of Hydon's Ball, on whose six-hundred-foot summit is a memorial seat dedicated to Octavia Hill, one of the founders of the National Trust.

8 WITLEY and MILFORD COMMONS

Take A3 south-west past Guildford. A mile beyond Milford, turn left on minor road (Webb Road) to car-park on the right. (This can also be reached down A286 from Godalming, turning right along Webb Road from the east.) There is a picnic site beside the car-park, a favourite haunt of butterflies. From here it is only a short stroll through the pine woods to a well-appointed information centre.

The centre is open 11 a.m.-1 p.m. and 1.45 p.m.-5 p.m. daily except Monday and Friday, April to October. Also open during same hours on Bank Holiday Mondays, and weekend afternoons in November. Car-park gates closed at 6 p.m. WC.

Graphic displays of local history and wildlife are a permanent feature, and at regular intervals each day there is an audio-visual programme. The shop supplies publications on conservation and the management of our countryside. Study groups may book in advance (Witley Common Information Centre, Witley, Godalming, Surrey) for a 2½-hour programme including an audio-visual session and guided tour of the commons. Individual visitors are free to make their own way along a sequence of waymarked trails, or simply to sprawl in the picnic areas and enjoy the sights, sounds and smells.

Enough history, political and horticultural, of Witley survives to make any of these wanderings a pleasure and a stimulus. There are Bronze Age burial mounds; and in Norman times the area was important enough to be recorded in some detail in Domesday Book. From that period until the time of Queen Elizabeth I it was part of a royal manor, and during and after that time its waters fed hammer ponds of the Wealden iron industry. After centuries as open heathland it was taken over in the First World War for use as army camps, and used again for military purposes during the Second World War. The focal point of both red and yellow waymarked routes is still referred to as the Parade Ground: after removal of the tarmac it was covered over with soil carted in from the Hog's Back between Guildford and Farnham, and it is now a great gathering place for summer butterflies. Crouching among the pines are anti-tank teeth.

The yellow waymarked trail is considered best for a first visit and also has the advantage of being negotiable by wheelchairs except after protracted wet weather – surely a familiar hazard in Britain. The red route, about two miles long, displays various aspects of heathland and woods of birch and pine, devised to illustrate management methods in contrast to the natural state of other areas. Near the Parade Ground the track seems surprisingly firm – due to the fact that the foundations of a road laid for Army use were not removed during the general demolition. Birds of several species are to be found here in spring, and at various times there are flowers such as wild parsnip, marjoram and centaury. Brambles beside the path have been introduced specifically to provide nectar for large numbers of insects. Human calculation was also responsible for the creation of a glade in which butterflies could flourish, and for tree clearance to prevent the drying-up of a bog over which now runs a wooden causeway.

The orange route starts on the other side of the road from Witley Common car-park entrance, running over Milford Common and offering a show of deliberately planned techniques in parts which have been invaded and recolonized by trees and shrubs not indigenous to the original, untreated acid soil. Part of this common was used as a baseball pitch by Canadian troops during the First World War, and there was another army camp here during the Second World War, some of whose huts were occupied by Polish civilian squatters before being demolished. Soil was brought in here as well as onto Witley Common to make good the surface, its contours still identifiable by the growths of different shrubs. A colony of blackberry bushes is thought to have been planted by the squatters.

More recently, in 1981, some minor disturbance was caused to the surface and what lay below it by the laying of an oil pipeline, its

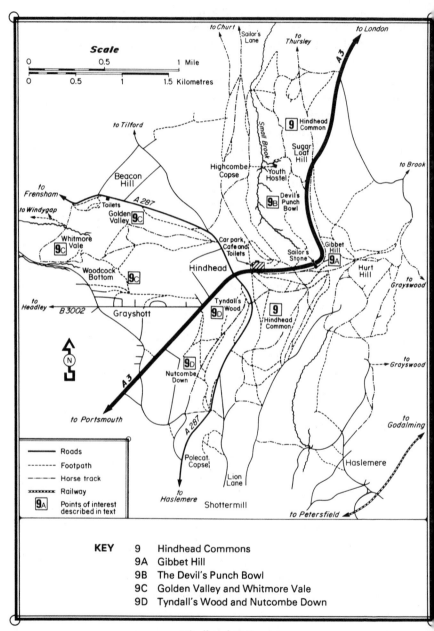

Hindhead Commons

path traceable beside a section of the orange trail. As the information centre's printed guide comments, the jumbo jet flying over the rambler on this common may have been supplied by the oil being pumped under his feet from Fawley to Gatwick. And there are faint traces of another, earlier route: a track which was once the old coaching road to the south-west, now superseded by the A3.

Running on from here, west of the A3, is Thursley Common, incorporating a large nature reserve. There are also hammer ponds, which worked iron forges until late in the eighteenth century.

9 HINDHEAD COMMONS

Take A3 past Guildford and through Milford towards Hindhead. At the end of its steep climb to the village, just before crossroads and traffic lights, there is a large car-park on the right. Refreshments. WC.

From the car-park there are trails on both sides of the main road through more than fourteen hundred acres of greensand hills, deep combes and plunging slopes of heather and pine. Trail guides and information leaflets are available from the car-park café.

Hindhead Commons were once nothing but bleak, windswept wasteland on this high upthrust of sandstone over which ran the main highway between London and Portsmouth before the days of the A3. Views now exhilarating in their unspoilt grandeur were once frightening to the lonely traveller. It was a happy place only for highwaymen and footpads. Today it has so much to offer the casual or more determined walker that some sub-division of this entry is essential.

9A Gibbet Hill

Starting on the crown of the hill, immediately across the A3 from the car-park, is Gibbet Hill waymarked nature trail. For a while it follows the original London to Portsmouth coaching route, between trees such as rowan, holly, oak and silver birch, and passes a former dewpond which has been restored by volunteers.

The path leads to a memorial stone recalling the murder of a sailor trudging over these heights in 1786. The inscription threatens a curse on anyone who tries to move the stone. Three men the sailor had met at Esher, to whom he had probably talked too freely, followed him, caught up with him on the heath and murdered him. They soon gave themselves away, trying to sell his clothes near Petersfield, and were tried and sentenced to death. The sailor's body lies in Thursley churchyard. The bodies of his killers hung for a long time in chains on Gibbet Hill, on the spot marked since 1851 with a Celtic cross. Part of the old gibbet is kept in Haslemere museum. Gibbet chains and informative pictures are displayed in the Royal Huts Hotel, once a solitary coaching inn dispensing hospitality on a barren hilltop.

Another feature introduced by man is an Ordnance Survey trigonometrical point at the second highest spot in Surrey – the highest being Leith Hill. A metal plate on top of the pillar gives directions and distances of visible landmarks. There are other lofty viewpoints at Hurt Hill (so named from the prevalent local 'hurts' or bilberries) and from the open heathland to the south and west; and traces can be found of another old road, the hollow track of the old turnpike between Haslemere and Thursley.

9B The Devil's Punch Bowl

This steep combe lies within the steep curve of the A3 as it climbs from Thursley towards Hindhead. It was known to Saxon settlers as the Wolf's Den, but by the nineteenth century William Cobbett, at first declaring it 'certainly the most villainous spot God ever made', came to the conclusion that he agreed with those ancestors who darkly 'ascribed its formation to another power'.

The deep natural arena was formed over the centuries by the action of water springing from the junction of sandstone and clay, eroding the land and creating patches of bog with their accompaniment of typical bog plants, overlooked by heather-covered sandy ridges and hummocks. Heavy rains running down the slopes continue the erosion and swell a stream which eventually feeds into the River Wey. Here and there can still be discerned the footings of old cottages occupied a couple of hundred years ago by countrymen who made brooms from the birch and heather and so were known as 'broom squires'.

A nature trail from the car-park, taking in all this, together with old farm tracks, hedges, pine, birch, oak and crab apple, and waterside alders, covers $2\frac{1}{2}$ miles or so.

9C Golden Valley, Woodcock Bottom and Whitmore Vale

These are reached within a couple of minutes from the car-park by turning right at the crossroads on A287 towards Churt and Farnham. There are footpaths through the woods and vales. WC to the left of the road at Beacon Hill, on the corner of Whitmore Vale. The delectable Golden Valley often rings to the call of the woodcock, hence the name of part of it – Woodcock Bottom.

9D Tyndall's Wood and Nutcombe Down

These lie immediately south-east of the A3 towards Portsmouth or can be reached from A287 towards Haslemere; or their footpaths can be picked up from those starting across the road from Hindhead car-park and crossing Hindhead Common. Between A287 and Lion Lane lies another locally named patch of woodland, this time with a touch of menace – Polecat Copse.

10 LUDSHOTT COMMON and WAGGONERS WELLS, near Hindhead

Take A3 past Guildford and through Hindhead. Half a mile beyond Hindhead crossroads turn right on westbound B3002 through Grayshott towards Headley. A short distance west of Grayshott is the Dunelm car-park, with trails leading out across Ludshott Common, around 650 acres of rolling heathland. This was an important sixteenth-century iron-founding district, and its string of pools, now forming one of the sources of the River Wey, were originally hammer ponds. The area was used as a tank training ground during the last war but bears few scars from those days.

Three attractive lakes shelter under the trees in a steeply cut vale. Known as Waggoners Wells, these can be reached from Ludshott Common or from Bramshott village by a lane past the old mill and the church, and then across the rewarding expanse of Bramshot Common.

Leaflets for Waggoners Wells nature trails and for one of the trails from Dunelm car-park can be obtained from the post office or newsagent in Grayshott.

NEARBY FEATURES:

Bohunt Manor, Liphook. Woodland gardens incorporating a

water garden, a lakeside walk, and a collection of more than a hundred ornamental ducks, geese and cranes. Open noon-5 p.m. daily, Monday to Friday. Small fee. WC.

Hollycombe House Steam Collection. Just over a mile south of Liphook on minor road towards Midhurst. Narrow-gauge railway through woodlands to views over the South Downs. Standard-gauge tramway with unique locomotive. Restored engine-room of paddle-steamer and other steam equipment. Traction-engine rides, woodland walks, fairground organ. Picnic area. Open noon-6 p.m. Sundays and Bank Holidays Easter to September; also Wednesday and Thursday in June and July, and Wednesday, Thursday and Saturday in August. Fee. Refreshments. Shop. WC.

11 WEY AND GODALMING NAVIGATION

Intercepting several of our suggested routes across this landscape are strands of the River Wey, the Wey Navigation, the Wey and Arun Canal, and Godalming Navigation. Lush meadows open out behind the alder trees lining the banks, and towpaths often coax the passer-by down to the water's edge or – sadly – to choked, dried-up channels. At several points along the healthier stretches there are organized river trips or pleasure craft for hire.

In the sixteenth century the River Wey was made navigable from Guildford to a junction with the Thames at Weybridge, and for a few centuries provided power for watermills along the route. Among survivors of these is the eighteenth-century town mill at Guildford. In 1760 the navigation was extended upstream to Godalming. During the Napoleonic Wars an attempt was made to open a direct waterway between London and the sea at Littlehampton, which necessitated linking two rivers by the Wey and Arun Canal from Newbridge to Shalford. By the time of its completion it was overtaken by improved roads and then by the railways. After long neglect, enthusiasts are working to reopen canal sections for recreational purposes.

There is interesting walking along several stretches of towpath from Weybridge (reached from M25 junction 11 by eastbound A317) to Guildford (A3 south-west from M25 junction 10). At Pyrford (A3 south-west from M25 junction 10, and turn right on northbound B367) there are extensive watermeadows near a large marina; and a footpath under Ockham Hill leads back towards the A3 and the Royal Horticultural Society Garden at Wisley (see Chapter 3). From Guildford a pleasant path accompanies the Godalming Navigation to Shalford and the open space of Shalford Park. The track crosses the Pilgrims' Way and North Downs Way at what used to be St Catherine's Ferry for transporting pilgrims across the river.

12 PETWORTH PARK

Take A3 south-west to Guildford, A3100 to Milford, and turn left on southbound A283 to Petworth.

The huge deer park around Petworth House, landscaped by 'Capability' Brown and much painted by Turner, is open daily, free, 9 a.m.-sunset. There are over seven hundred acres for strolling, playing and picnicking, but dogs must be kept on a lead, and no cars are allowed in the grounds. There is a car-park beside A283 as one approaches the town. A car-park for visitors to the house and gardens lies within the main entrance gate in the town.

Petworth House (NT) is a late-seventeenth-century mansion with a frontage 320 feet long. Inside, one of the state rooms was decorated by Grinling Gibbons in an efflorescence of limewood fruit, flowers, birds, beasts and musical instruments. There are important collections of pictures including many by Turner, who was provided with a studio here by his patron Lord Egremont – the man also responsible for raising the money for the Wey and Arun Canal (see preceding entry).

House and pleasure grounds, with some superb trees, are open 2 p.m.-6 p.m. daily except Monday and Friday (but open Bank Holiday Monday and closed followed Tuesday) April to the end of October. Fee. Refreshments. WC.

For an alternative return route, take westbound A272 towards Midhurst. There is a large picnic site north of the road, beside a minor road about a mile east of Midhurst. In Easebourne turn right on northbound A286 through Haslemere and rejoin homeward-bound A3100 at Milford.

13 HOG'S BACK PICNIC SITE

Take A3 south-west past Guildford and pick up westbound A31 towards Farnham along the high ridge of the Hog's Back. The parking and picnic site is on the left, just beyond the turn-off for Godalming. Note that there is no direct access from the eastbound dual carriageway.

This is a wide, generously long grassy site flanking the road, backed by small clumps of woodland. There is an ample spread of picnic tables and benches, and if you have omitted to bring your own provisions and cooler bag with you, there is no need for recrimination: the refreshment kiosk serves hot and cold food and drinks. Along the southern scarp of the Hog's Back runs the Pilgrims' Way, in fact a Bronze Age track long before the medieval worshippers trod this route. All of its users, in any bygone century, would surely have been pleased if such a resting-place and such facilities had existed then.

NEARBY FEATURE:

Compton. The village is signposted from the turn-off for Godalming, just before the picnic site described above. In Down Lane are two buildings dedicated to the life and work of the painter and sculptor G.F. Watts. His devoted widow built a well-lit gallery for the display of his works, including portraits of Lillie Langtry and of his first wife, the actress Ellen Terry, and also a towering, eccentric mortuary chapel in a colourful mish-mash of Romanesque, Celtic, Pre-Raphaelite and *art nouveau* styles – an absolute stunner of florid absurdity. The art gallery is open free every afternoon except Thursday from 2 p.m., plus Wednesday and Saturday mornings 11 a.m.-1 p.m.; the chapel is open daily until dusk.

14 ROWHILL NATURE RESERVE, near Farnham

Take A3 south-west past Guildford and pick up westbound A31 to Farnham, then northbound A325 towards Aldershot.

Administered by local conservationists, the fifty acres of heath and woodland, with a peat bog and three streams, are open at all times to careful visitors who enjoy walking in natural surroundings. A Field Centre building at Cranmore Lane entrance to the reserve is open to the public 2.30 p.m.-4.30 p.m. on Sundays.

15 CROOKSBURY HILL, Tilford

Take A3 south-west past Guildford, A31 to Farnham, and B3001 towards Milford, with the River Wey meandering round the romantic ruins of Waverley Abbey close to the road. Minor roads to the left lead north over Crooksbury Common and to Crooksbury Hill. There is good walking on the common, and the conical, sandy hill has long been one of the favourite picnic spots in the neighbourhood. Puttenham Common also offers plenty of open space to the north-east and has two car-parks: one reached from Puttenham village by a lane signposted to Elstead and Cut Mill, the other about a mile further on near the Cut Mill crossroads.

Alternative approach: from the Hog's Back section of A31, as above, turn left on B3000 signposted for Godalming, turn right into Puttenham village, and use one of the car-parks described above as base for the various stretches of common.

NEARBY FEATURE:

Old Kiln Museum. North of Reeds Road between Tilford village and A287 at Frensham. Moderate entrance fee (half-price for children). Free parking and picnic areas, imaginatively planned agricultural museum with an arboretum and woodland walk, train rides for children on Sundays, and a reconstructed working forge which is used to make or repair parts needed in the museum. A hop press recalls the days when this was a major hop-growing region. There are displays, housed in old farm buildings, of Victorian household and nursery souvenirs, veterinary equipment, and a dairy, a pharmacy, and a shepherd's hut.

Open 11 a.m.-6 p.m. Wednesday to Sunday and Bank Holidays, April to the end of the September. WC.

16 FRENSHAM PONDS and COUNTRY PARK

Take A3 south-west past Guildford, A31 to Farnham, and southbound A287 towards Hindhead. The road cuts across the sand and scrub of Frensham Common, with Frensham Great Pond to the right and Frensham Little Pond to the left towards Tilford.

The heath, with large parking spaces close to the road, rises to a line of three substantial bowl barrows known as the Devil's Jumps.

The largest of these, Stony Jump, has a path up which one can scramble to the summit, offering sweeping views towards the Hog's Back and over Sussex and Hampshire.

The Great Pond is one of the largest lakes in southern England, and nobody could call the Little Pond truly little. It has its own large car-park a mile along a minor road to the east of the A287. Both lakes are ideal for fishing and sailing; but local societies have a lien on both the angling and the sailing.

There is parking for the Great Pond west of A287, and on the far bank of this pond, just off a minor road leading round it from A287 past the church, is parking for the heathland and waterside walks of the country park. Refreshment kiosk and Red Cross post. WC.

In St Mary's Church, Frensham, is preserved what is claimed to be a genuine witch's cauldron, a good three feet in diameter. A deep cave near Waverley Abbey was traditionally the home of a crone called Mother Ludlam, who made loans of her magic-making possessions to those who came and asked for them – provided always that these were returned without fail within two days. Another version of the story ascribes this custom to fairies on Borough Hill. Either way, somebody once transgressed and, having borrowed the cauldron, failed to return it. Mother Ludlam – or the fairies – refused ever to lend anything again, and after a period in Waverley Abbey the cauldron reached Frensham church.

Alternative approach: begin route as above but, instead of transferring to A31, stay on A3 to Milford. There either take westbound B3001 to Elstead and turn south on minor roads over Elstead Common and Churt Common to join A287 just south of Frensham Great Pond, or continue south-west on A3 and turn off on westbound minor road through Thursley and over Churt Common to A287. (See also earlier entries for Milford, Witley and Thursley Commons.)

17 BLACK DOWN, near Haslemere

Take A3 past Guildford to Milford, and there pick up the southbound A286 across Witley Common and Grayswood Common to Haslemere.

The poet Alfred, Lord Tennyson, lived on the outskirts of Haslemere for a quarter of a century. His name is commemorated in

Tennyson's Lane, leading a mile south-east of the town to Black Down, on the eastern slope of which he built a house called Aldworth. The 918-foot summit of the hill is the highest point in Sussex, commanding a view over the Weald which inspired Tennyson to write of 'Green Sussex fading into blue, with one grey glimpse of sea'.

Stone Age settlers on this height left many of their worked flints for later folk to find. In Elizabethan times it served as one of a chain of warning beacons. Today, its several hundred acres of wooded slope and heathland tempt the visitor into a richness of heather, oak, birch and Scots pine, with some especially fine beeches on the east. A few small ponds have surrounds of moss and bog plants. A leaflet describing a 1½-mile nature trail can be obtained from Haslemere museum or bookshops in the town; but free and easy explorations of the woods offer just as much satisfaction.

Names of villages, lanes and plantations all around recall the old days of the flourishing iron industry: Hammer Patches, Furnace Wood, Minepit Close.

Alternative approach: proceed as above to Milford, but then continue on A3 to Hindhead (see earlier entry), turn left at Hindhead crossroads on southbound A287, and follow signs into Haslemere.

18 MARLEY COMMON, near Haslemere

Take either of preceding suggested routes into Haslemere, then continue on southbound A286 to Kingsley Green. In the village turn right on minor road to Marley Common and its steep woodlands.

There is a delightful complex of wooded hills and clefts here: Marley Common and Wood, Kingsley Green Common, Marley Coombe and Marley Heights with its viewpoints known as The Terraces. By the war memorial just north of B2131 are Shottermill Ponds, two impressive hammer ponds now calm and happily retired from their labours.

Alternative approach: take either of preceding suggested routes into Haslemere, then pick up westbound B2131 past Shottermill Ponds to minor southbound roads on the left across Linchmere Common with its footpaths towards Marley and Fernhurst.

FROM JUNCTION

11

Note: All the following routes can also be joined from junction 10 by means of A3 south-west to Guildford.

19 ALICE HOLT FOREST, near Farnham

Take southbound A320 through Woking to Guildford and pick up westbound A31 to Farnham. Take southbound A325 towards Petersfield. The forest is signposted about three miles out of Farnham town centre.

From the Halfway House inn at Bucks Horn Oak turn left on the Dockenfield road. The entrance to the main car-park is three hundred yards along on the left, with a short path to the Forestry Commission's Visitor Information Centre. WC. Another car-park can be reached from this same entrance by a short forest drive to Lodge Pond.

Alice Holt was not, as might be supposed, some local lady of the manor or benefactress. In Saxon times the woodlands which then belonged to Bishop Aelfsige of Winchester were named by him Aelfsige's Holt (or Wood), which over the years has been corrupted to its present form. Roman potteries existed here before the Saxons; after them, in Norman times it was a royal hunting forest. Later it supplied 'wooden walls' for the fleet both in Tudor times and in the early nineteenth century, when Inclosures were made to facilitate 'the better cultivation of Navy timber'. Today its 2,500 acres are managed by the Forestry Commission, who, in addition to cropping its timber as required, have established a number of nature trails and informal paths and laid out picnic places in glades near the car-parks.

The information centre mounts displays of forest history and modern uses, offers full details of facilities for the casual visitor and educational groups, and has leaflets and maps for sale, including those outlining the main trails.

Walks incorporating the banks and picnic sites of Lodge Pond and Willow Green begin at the centre. A 'Habitat Trail' starts from a car-park on the opposite side of the Dockenfield road, a short distance south-east of the information centre entrance. Here in the Abbotts Wood Inclosure is a varied habitat of trees and plants, with open glades and rides to add shifting light and shadow to the picture. Birds and roe deer move in and out, wild flowers flourish, and well over twenty species of butterfly have been identified here. The deer are descendants of those who were once so enthusiastically hunted through the forest.

Goose Green Inclosure is reached by returning to A325 at Bucks Horn Oak and crossing it onto minor road opposite. The car-park is a short distance along on the left. Here again is a picnic site, with a number of winding paths making off through the trees and dappled glades. A 'History Trail' is its special feature, dealing with past events rather than the nature and cultivation of the forest. At one point a Roman-style pottery kiln has been rebuilt and is occasionally set to work under stringent safety conditions by archaeologists studying Roman methods.

Saxon and Norman monarchs set great store by their 'vert and venison' – trees and deer – and laid down severe punishments for those who dared to poach or even gather kindling in royal forests. In Henry VIII's time the demands of the Navy had become more important than any sporting activity, however regal, and a lodge was set up for a Goose Green forester, one of a group who seem to have lived very well off local produce: this officer kept cattle for himself in a patch of fenced-in parkland, while a number of fishponds were installed to supply the chief officer at Alice Holt Lodge.

This lodge stands in another of the sections separated from its original neighbours by enclosure and then by local roads, including the Farnham to Petersfield turnpike which has now become the A325. An entrance is to be found on the west of the northbound A325 towards Farnham, and past the lodge there is parking close to the arboretum.

NEARBY FEATURE:

At Holts Pound just before entering Alice Holt Forest from the Farnham direction there is a large car-park with a grassy picnic area on the right (west) side of A325. Beside it are Birdworld and Underwaterworld. Over a thousand birds, including vultures, parrots and wildfowl, are on display in extensive gardens with other picnic areas, shelters, a children's playground and a 'fun and fitness' trail for adults. There is also a separate aquarium building by the car-park. Fee.

Open 9.30 a.m. daily except Christmas Day. Refreshments. W.C.

20 SELBORNE COMMON

Take southbound A320 through Woking to Guildford and pick up westbound A31 through Farnham and onto Alton bypass. Turn left on B3006 to Selborne.

It was here that the eighteenth-century cleric and naturalist the Reverend Gilbert White recorded his observations on local wildlife and in 1789 published the *Natural History and Antiquities of Selborne*. He helped to make the zigzag path to the top of Selborne Hanger, from which one can look down on the delightful prospect of the village and its environs much as he knew them. At the summit is a monolith known as the Wishing Stone. Everywhere the beech woods are beautiful, but especially along the wooded slopes of the Long and Short Lythes.

The Wakes, the author's old home in the village itself, now houses two museums. One is devoted to White and his work, with rooms furnished in the style of his time and containing many of his own possessions, as well as a range of family portraits. The upper floor of the building is the Oates Memorial Library and Museum in honour of two explorers – Frank Oates, nineteenth-century naturalist who died on an expedition in southern Africa, and his nephew Captain Lawrence Oates, famous for his part in Scott's ill-fated Antarctic venture. The large garden, planted in eighteenth-century style, is open to museum visitors.

Museums open noon-5.30 p.m. daily except Monday (but open Bank Holidays) March to October. Fee. WC.

NEARBY FEATURE:

Jane Austen's house, Chawton. Reached from Selborne by B3006 north-west towards Alton, and just before junction with A31 a left turn on minor road into Chawton. The author's home is now a small museum in the village street. Visitors may picnic in the garden.

Open daily 11 a.m.-4.30 p.m. (except Mondays and Tuesdays from November to March, Christmas Day and Boxing Day). Fee. Shop. WC.

Alternative approach: from Farnham take southbound A325 through Alice Holt Forest and Woolmer Forest. Just beyond Greatham turn right on B3006 north-west to Selborne. In reverse this could make an agreeable return route as an alternative to the A31.

21 QUEEN ELIZABETH COUNTRY PARK, near Petersfield

Take southbound A320 through Woking to Guildford and there pick up A3 south-west through Petersfield. About two miles south of the town is the country park, covering hundreds of acres both sides of the road. There is a forest drive through extensive beech woods, with picnic glades and car-parks, as well as a number of barbecue sites. Grass-skis can be hired on summer Sundays. WC.

The Park Centre offers information, a selection of maps, guides and other books, craft displays, a cinema and a café. The centre is open daily from March to October, and on Sundays from November to February. The park itself is open free all year round, with a small charge for parking only. Although it lies on the extreme limit of our region, it should come close to the top of anybody's list of ideal days' outings.

22 BUTSER ANCIENT FARM, near Petersfield

This is set beside the A3 south of Petersfield and forms part of the Queen Elizabeth Country Park (see preceding entry); but it should be dealt with separately in view of its distinct opening times and charges.

Planned as a 'Celtic Experience', the farm re-creates Iron Age life 2,000 years ago, with a roundhouse and a working industrial zone including shaft and bowl furnaces, roasting pits and casting moulds. There are pottery kilns of prehistoric and later Roman types, and on certain weekends demonstrations of ploughing, cooking, weaving and spinning. Open weekdays 2 p.m.-6 p.m., Sundays 10 a.m.-6 p.m., April to September. Fee. Parking, refreshments and other facilities as for the country park.

12-16

The River Thames indulges in some capricious twists and turns in its upper reaches, flowing down from its two headstreams in the Cotswolds to create a watery main road, busy with traffic in spite of its contortions and the hold-ups at its numerous locks. Unlike the motorways, this thoroughfare no longer carries much in the way of freight: its main travellers are those in search of pleasure. Locks devised for practical purposes are now also meeting-places for amiable chat. The leisurely pedestrian on the towpath can choose any one of dozens of places to sit and contemplate the colour and activity ... and also the long moments of tranquillity on and beside the water. Whole days could be spent in walking along the river bank from one parking spot to another.

For those on the move, by car or on foot, the twisting ribbon is continually glinting into view, offering a vista from a hillside or bridge, perhaps at its best snaking between Henley, Marlow and Maidenhead, curving past splendid Hambleden Mill and under the hanging woods of Cliveden.

In complete contrast to these banks and watermeadows are the sandy heathlands of Surrey, running on from our south-western chapter, some overrun by the army and frequently flying red flags to warn of shooting on the ranges, others surprisingly free and remote, with picnic places and woodland walks; and, both by the river and in the parklands, there are the historic mansions of those who wished to be close to their London interests yet stylishly apart from them.

KEY

1 Windsor Great Park
2 Lightwater Country Park, Bagshot
3 Chobham Common
4 Horsell Common, Woking
5 Yateley Common Country Park, near Blackwater
6 Blackwater Valley
7 Bracknell
8 California Country Park, near Wokingham
9 Staines Reservoirs
10 Thorpe Park, near Chertsey
11 Black Park, near Slough
12 Langley Park, near Slough
13 Maidenhead Thicket
14 The Hockett Picnic Site, near Cookham Dean
15 Cookham and Maidenhead Commons
16 Hurley
17 Dinton Pastures Country Park, near Reading
18 Wellington Country Park, near Reading
19 Hazely Heath, near Hartley Wintney
20 Child Beale Wildlife Trust, near Pangbourne
21 Mapledurham Country Park, near Reading
22 Well Place Bird Farm, Ipsden
23 Bayhurst Wood Country Park, near Uxbridge
24 Burnham Beeches, near Slough
25 Wooburn Green Picnic Site, near Beaconsfield
26 Hambleden, near Henley-on-Thames

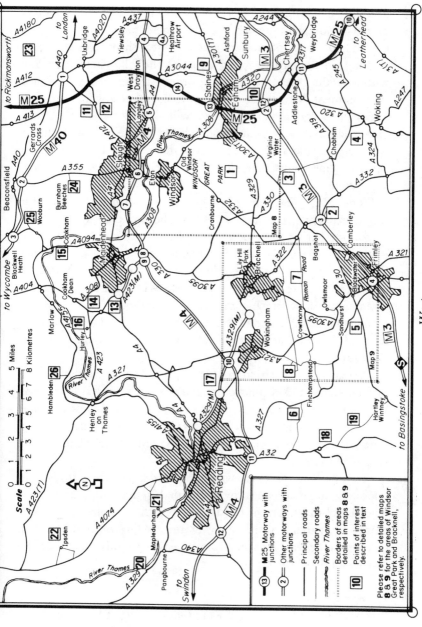

West

1 WINDSOR GREAT PARK

The different features of the park and its immediate surroundings cannot be lumped together in a few general paragraphs under the heading of one particular junction. Its sheer extent makes recommended approach routes difficult. The following entries deal with individual sites in a clockwise order – though it is not implied for a moment that anyone will want to complete a whole circuit in one visit – and obviously much will depend on drivers' own preferences and the direction from which they are coming. Windsor is so famous and so well signposted that explicit instructions are perhaps superfluous; but for the newcomer, here are a few suggestions.

From M25 junction 13 take A308 north-west. To visit Runnymede first, continue on A308, then to pick up clockwise route turn left on southbound A328 and pick up A30 south of Englefield Green. For the Savill and Valley Gardens, Virginia Water, and parking places within the park, take A30 south-west (if preferred, A30 can be taken direct from M25 junction 13, leaving Runnymede until later); turn right on westbound A329 towards Sunninghill and Ascot; and to follow the western edge of the park, turn right on northbound B383 and join A332 across the park into Windsor.

Alternative approach: from M25 junction 15 take westbound M4 to Slough. From M4 junction 6 follow signs southwards towards Windsor, then take either A308 to Runnymede (a road offering one of the most famous views of Windsor Castle to the left up the Long Ride), or A332 south-west – i.e. in reverse order from the preceding suggested route.

Major parking spaces are well signposted beside these roads. It is important to come well provided with 10p and 50p pieces: even when entry to gardens or parkland is free, there is often a nominal charge for parking which involves the feeding of coin-operated barriers on the way in or out. To compensate for this, many parking patches on the grass verges are free.

1A *Runnymede*

It was to these meadows that King John, staying at Windsor, came reluctantly to meet his rebellious barons, who had been lodging in Staines, and put his seal on Magna Carta, the great charter of

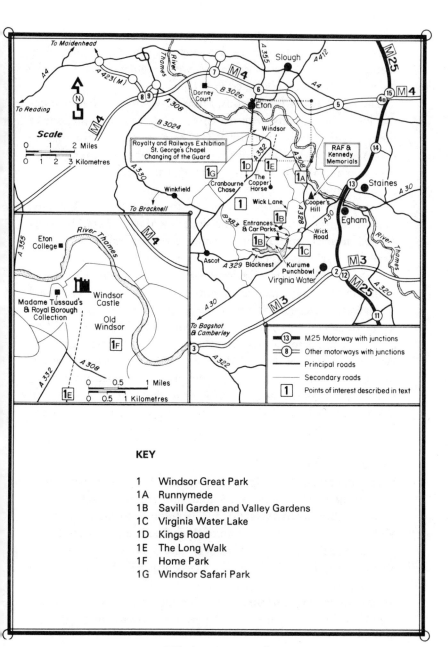

KEY

1   Windsor Great Park
1A Runnymede
1B Savill Garden and Valley Gardens
1C Virginia Water Lake
1D Kings Road
1E The Long Walk
1F Home Park
1G Windsor Safari Park

Windsor Great Park

English liberties.

In the late eighteenth century there was a racecourse here, conveniently close to the royal residence in Windsor. Both King George IV and King William IV were regular patrons of the meetings. They were abolished in 1886.

The A308 across the meadows runs between two commemorative kiosks or columns, with matching lodges to either side, one of them housing a tea-room and WC. There are several free parking spaces on the wide grassy fringes of the river, one of them also with tea-room and WC. Boat trips depart regularly from a mooring just below the memorial columns.

Footpaths climb Cooper's Hill to other monuments. A domed classical temple at the foot of the slope is a Magna Carta Memorial erected from contributions by nine thousand members of the American Bar Association in a tribute to the charter's principle of 'Freedom under Law'. Halfway up the hill is another, sadder testimony to Anglo-American friendship: an 'acre of English ground … given to the United States by the people of Britain' as the site of a memorial to the assassinated President John F. Kennedy. And on the crest, commanding a superb panorama of the Thames valley and Windsor, is the Air Forces Memorial in honour of over twenty thousand airmen who have no known grave. For those not wishing to toil up the incline, a car-park closer to the Air Forces Memorial can be reached up A328 from the junction just north of the meadows, with a signposted turn-off to the left of this road.

1B Savill Garden and Valley Gardens

Both gardens are well signposted off the A30 about half a mile south of its junction with A328, and both are most easily reached from this turn down Wick Road. The entrance to the car-park for Valley Gardens is at the junction of Wick Road and Wick Lane; that for the Savill Garden, a short way along Wick Lane from the junction. Admission to the Valley Gardens is free, but the drive to the car-park is via a coin-operated barrier. The Savill Garden also has a barrier, coin-operated when leaving; but those paying the admission fee to this garden will be given a token to operate the exit without charge.

During the late eighteenth and early nineteenth centuries the unkempt heaths and bogs of Windsor Great Park were landscaped by two successive Dukes of Cumberland. In 1932 the posts of Deputy Surveyor and later of Deputy Ranger were filled by Eric Savill, who set about creating a new complex of landscaped gardens around what at the time was merely an estate nursery. His work so impressed King George VI that in 1951 he decreed that what had somewhat unpoetically been known as the Bog Garden should be renamed the Savill Garden; and in 1955 the Deputy Ranger was knighted by Queen Elizabeth II and went on to become Director of Gardens until his retirement in 1970. He died ten years later.

Today the garden should, strictly speaking, be referred to in the plural, since there is such an entrancing sequence of differing layouts. Peat gardens, woodland, herbaceous borders and the delectable willow garden all have distinctive characteristics of their own. The willow garden is at its most radiant in spring, the herbaceous borders in late summer; but every attempt is made to ensure what can only be called an orchestration of differing yet harmonious colours between late June and October. There are rose bushes and climbers, an Alpine meadow, azaleas and rhododendrons, and alluring avenues of flowerbeds and shrubs leading on to wide paths through the woodland. Near a beech wood, the Jubilee Garden and a new bridge over the lower of two ponds were opened to commemorate Queen Elizabeth II's Silver Jubilee in 1978.

Open daily 10 a.m.-6 p.m. (7 p.m. at weekends) or sunset; but closed 25-28 December. Fee. Licensed restaurant open March to October. Shop with herbs and plants for sale. WC.

From Savill Garden, a tree-shaded footpath leads about a mile to Valley Gardens, so that the same car-park can be used for both, provided one does not mind the two-mile walk there and back.

The Valley Gardens also owe their present appearance to Sir Eric Savill, who turned his attention to clearance of the undergrowth which had choked the place during the Second World War. A First World War gravel pit became a heather garden; new plantations were established around original eighteenth-century plantings; new breeds of rhododendron were introduced from south-east Asia, and many hybrids were developed, to form the largest collection of rhododendron species in the world; and hydrangeas seem to take over the whole area in the summer. But above all an atmosphere of informality has been maintained, to provide a contrast to some of the more formal layouts of Savill Garden; though, like their neighbour, the Valley Gardens manage to provide something of beauty at almost any time of the year.

1C Virginia Water Lake

The plushy houses of the village lie east of the A30, but the water itself is to the west, with a clearly marked car-park by the Wheatsheaf hotel on the A30, and Blacknest car-park beside the westbound A329.

This artificial lake was created from marshy streams in the middle of the eighteenth century by landscape gardeners Paul and Thomas Sandby to the instructions of the Duke of Cumberland, the 'Butcher' Cumberland of murderous repute. South of A329, towards Sunningdale, the same duke built himself a folly tower in 1750 to display his collection of cannon. It was later converted into a house for George IV, and in the present century was the favourite residence of the Prince of Wales, uncrowned King Edward VIII and later Duke of Windsor.

The surroundings of Virginia Water form an agreeable neighbour to the above-mentioned Valley Gardens, whose avenue of Canadian conifers runs down to its northern bank, where there stands a totem pole a hundred feet high commemorating the centenary of British Columbia in 1958. Far more ancient, on the southern side is a colonnade from Leptis Magna in Tripoli, re-erected in 1827 by George IV's architect Sir Jeffry Wyattville. The shape of the lake is so distinctive that during the Second World War it was drained so that it would not provide a navigational aid for German bombers.

1D Kings Road

This, the A332, offers a wide view across airy expanses of parkland to the castle and town. There are numerous free parking and picnic spaces on hard ground and grass on the fringe of Cranbourne Chase, west of the road.

1E The Long Walk

A three-mile, tree-lined avenue stretching from the King George IV gateway of the castle across the A308 and on towards the Copper Horse, a statue of King George III erected in 1831.

1F Home Park
A wide grassy public space between the castle and the river, scene of
many local festivities.

1G Windsor Safari Park
Adapting the foregoing suggested routes, either take B3022
south-west from Windsor or, approaching from Virginia Water and
Blacknest via A329 and B383, continue on B383 and veer right
through Cranbourne Chase on B3022. The safari park is well
signposted at each major junction. Price of admission includes free
coach services around the area, drives through wild animal reserves,
lions and tigers, children's amusements, a 'soft play area' and
visiting acts of one kind and another during the summer season.
  Open daily 10 a.m. except Christmas Day. Fee. Refreshments.
Large picnic areas. WC.

NEARBY FEATURES:
Windsor Castle. Precincts open free daily. State apartments,
Queen Mary's dolls' house and St George's Chapel open (fee) at
varying times throughout the year, which should be checked in
advance. Closed when the Queen is in residence and on special
ceremonial occasions.
Madame Tussaud's Royalty and Empire exhibition. Just below
the castle, Windsor and Eton Central Station houses a huge
collection of waxworks depicting the arrival of Queen Victoria
by royal train, an audio-visual show, and a collection of local
Victoriana. Open daily 9.30 a.m.-5.30 p.m. except Christmas
Day. Fee. Shop. WC.
Dorney Court. From B3022 in Eton, north of Windsor, take
westbound B3026 to Dorney. Entrance to Dorney Court on sharp
curve in the village. One of the finest Tudor manor houses in
England, set in a beautiful surround of garden and hedges, and lived
in by the same family for nearly four hundred years. Superb great
hall and rooms full of old furniture, needlework and family por-
traits. Cream teas; shop selling home-grown vegetables and honey.
  Open 2 p.m.-5.30 p.m. all Easter weekend, then Sundays and
Bank Holiday Mondays until the second Sunday in October.
Sundays, Mondays and Tuesdays from June until September.
Fee. WC.

2 LIGHTWATER COUNTRY PARK, Bagshot

Take westbound M3 towards Basingstoke. At M3 junction 3 turn south on A322 and almost immediately turn right on minor road signposted Lightwater. A short distance into the village turn right on the Avenue, signposted Lightwater Country Park. Ample parking and picnic space. WC.

The park has an enclosed sports centre, lakes, tennis courts, a 'fitness circuit' with various barriers and hazards to surmount, long and short walks and nature trails. One climbing, undulating path links a number of especially attractive viewpoints above the surrounding heathland.

Bagshot Heath was once a haunt of highwaymen. Today it is an inviting stretch of gorse, heather, and fir and pine woods, sometimes busy with 'cycle-cross', or cross-country cycling events. Distant background noise comes occasionally from the famous ranges on Bisley Common to the south-west.

Alternative approach: from M25 junction 13 take A30 south-west, turn south on A322 through Bagshot, and right on minor road as above.

3 CHOBHAM COMMON, near Chobham and Bagshot

Take westbound M3 towards Basingstoke. At M3 junction 3 turn north on A322 through Bagshot and then right on A30 north-east towards Staines. Just past railway station turn right on southbound B383 towards Chobham.

The common, sprawling on both sides of the M3 motorway, with a tunnel under the road for the benefit of walkers, rises and falls unevenly over tracts of heath and scrub, with a few stray trees struggling for survival on little mounds or in sheltered gulleys. Locally known for generations as 'The Wastes', the area has a dour moorland atmosphere more often associated with the wild fells and tussocks of Durham and Northumberland. There are any number of informal parking spaces from which to explore the rugged heathland, with its paths and bridleways as tangled as its undergrowth. (Riding, it should be noted, is by permit only.) A particularly large car-park set at the junction of B383 and B386 offers plenty of good rough walking beyond.

Before Aldershot assumed its present status as the main British Army centre, Chobham Common was much used as a military training ground. A stone pillar on a mound a short distance from the main car-park commemorates the occasion in 1853 when Queen Victoria reviewed some eight thousand troops before they set off for the Crimea.

To appreciate the common at its best and to make a good choice of stopping-places, leave the B383/386 junction by the eastbound B386, and at the next roundabout turn right over M3 bridge towards Chobham, then sharp right immediately onto westbound minor road. There are parking and picnic sites with tables and benches on ragged ground to the right of this road, one of them set below a sandy hillock which looks like some ancient hill fort. Chobham Clump, a ring of trees like a miniature Chanctonbury Ring, once dominated the landscape here; but one night someone came out in darkness with a chainsaw and, for no known reason, cut them down. A few hundred yards down the road, a parking space on the left stands above another earthwork. Paths and bridleways lead off into mazes of bracken, scrub and wild flowers – scenery sometimes dark under lowering clouds, sometimes aglow with autumn hues. From stumpy heights and ragged ridges the views across heath and hill are marred only by the flicker and thunder of M3 traffic cutting a gash through this once remote wilderness.

Continuing on this road to rejoin the A383, turn left towards Chobham and left again on a minor road. Just beyond a sharp right-angled turn beside Gracious Pond farm, a parking and picnic site is set so secretively back in the trees that one needs to drive slowly and be alert for the entrance. From this secluded setting there are shaded walks through deep woodland.

Alternative approach: from M25 junction 13 take westbound A30 towards Bagshot; in Sunningdale turn south on B383 towards Chobham, then follow directions as above.

4 HORSELL COMMON, Woking

This runs on from Chobham Common (see preceding entry) across A3046 south-east of Chobham. A path across it leads through the trees to the towpath of the old canal which used to run forty miles from Basingstoke to Byfleet but now ends up at the Greywell tunnel entrance near Hook. Although the waterway is no longer navigable, the towpath can be walked the whole distance.

5 YATELEY COMMON COUNTRY PARK, near Blackwater

Take westbound M3 towards Basingstoke. At M3 junction 4 turn north on A321 towards Blackwater, and at roundabout turn left on westbound A30. A mile and a half along the road, shortly after the beginning of the dual carriageway section, there are two large parking and picnic sites set back from the eastbound carriageway and not easily identifiable at speed. Access is by gaps in the central reservation; or one can, more safely, continue to the Yateley roundabout and come back along the eastbound carriageway, when the sites will be on the left.

There are walks through the woods, several picnic areas, and in the western section a model boat pond. The region is incorporated in a sequence of regular guided walks from the Green, Yateley, as part of the Blackwater Valley Project (see following entry).

Alternative approach: from M25 junction 13 take A30 south-west through Bagshot towards Basingstoke, and beyond Blackwater follow instructions as above.

6 BLACKWATER VALLEY

Rowhill Nature Reserve (see Chapter 4) and Yateley (see preceding entry) are among the features encompassed by the Blackwater Valley Project, sponsored by local authorities, the Sports Council and the Countryside Commission. The aim is to clear up damage done over the years by residential and industrial encroachment and to stimulate public awareness of the beauties and scientific interest of the lands beside the River Blackwater.

In 1979 work began on restoring the original character of the landscape, revitalizing derelict land, establishing footpaths and planting thousands of trees and shrubs. Throughout coming years it is hoped there will be a steady expansion of activities such as angling, walking, canoeing, sailing and riding. Details of the times and routes of conducted tours of different sections can be obtained in advance from the Planning Department, Rushmoor Borough Council, but there is no reason why visitors should not explore the countryside themselves from parking spaces such as those by Farnham Park (beside A287), Lakeside Road in Aldershot (near both the River Blackwater and the Basingstoke canal), Rowhill Nature Reserve (as above), Yateley (as above), Farley Hill (off A327 between Yateley and Reading) and the Blackwater Valley Park.

This last-named park lies close to Admiralty Way off A321 just south of junction with A30 on the outskirts of Blackwater.

FROM JUNCTION

13

7 BRACKNELL

Take A30 south-west. On outskirts of Bagshot turn north-west on A322 towards Bracknell.

The town itself is one of those designated urban growths such as Crawley and Milton Keynes which since the Second World War have overlaid earlier villages with new office blocks, multi-storey car-parks, shopping precincts and housing estates. It has still, however, not swallowed up a large area of heath and forest to the south and east, and both the District Council and the Forestry Commission have tried to maintain reasonable recreational access to some of the more attractive walks and clearings. A ramblers' route devised in collaboration with the Ramblers' Association is waymarked through woods, beside farmland and over parks managed by the local authority, with plenty of picnic sites.

As well as informal car-parking spaces beside various roads through the region there are parking areas specially established to give access to main points of interest along the ramblers' footpath, and allow the visitor to take in just a short stretch of the walk if the full circuit proves too rigorous to contemplate. A selection of car-parks in the different areas is suggested below.

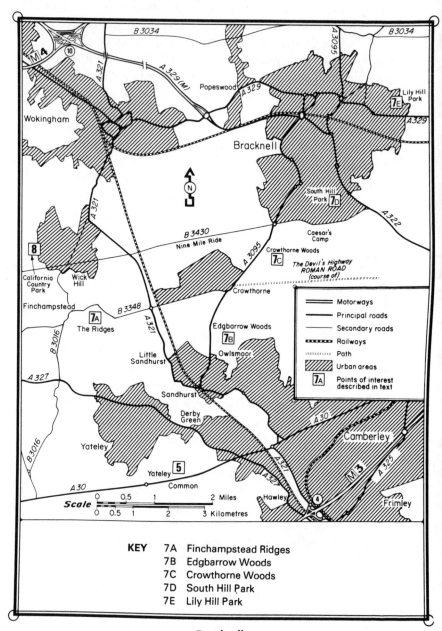

KEY   7A Finchampstead Ridges
       7B Edgbarrow Woods
       7C Crowthorne Woods
       7D South Hill Park
       7E Lily Hill Park

Bracknell

7A Finchampstead Ridges

Not strictly part of the district but firmly linked to it by the Nine Mile Ride (B3430) cutting through the woods and closing in on the town from the south, and by the straight track of old Roman road known as the Devil's Highway. Just off B3348 west of the A321 roundabout near Crowthorne station there is parking for the Ridges, some sixty acres of wooded ridge and heather. At the southern edge is a topograph identifying features of the landscape beyond.

Set in one patch of woodland is the Heath Pool, which can be reached by the Devil's Highway or a track known as Hollybush Ride; and from the pool is a path to the mixed species of quiet little Simons Wood.

7B Edgbarrow Woods

From the car-park near Crowthorne station it is possible to follow footpaths across the East Berks golf course or through the grounds of Wellington College; but for the woods proper it is better to make use of the car-park beside A3095 in Edgbarrow Woods. Almost eighty acres of heath and woodland here are intended for public recreation and provide a large picnic area.

Most of the pine and birch woodland, bog and heath lie within a designated Site of Special Scientific Interest. Some of the plant colonies could well be four thousand years old, though the woodlands on the higher ground are more recent plantings or have of their own accord encroached on former patches of heathland. Butterflies and moths are numerous, feeding off the heather and gorse. Owlsmoor Bog and its grasses form a contrast which makes the whole site well worth studying, with its mixture of wet and dry heathland together with coniferous woodland.

One of the paths established through the area may also be used as a jogging track and links up with a path from Edgbarrow Sports Centre, where there are changing facilities.

7C Crowthorne Woods

The easiest access to these is from the Nine Mile Ride, B3430, east of the A3095 roundabout just south of Bracknell. This road is sometimes said to have acquired its name in the time of Queen Anne, who suffered from gout but was anxious to follow the course of huntsmen through Windsor Forest, of which this was all once a part, and so decreed the laying out of a special route for her. Others ascribe it to a similar need in the case of King George III.

A small car-park is provided below Caesar's Camp, an Iron Age plateau fort with a name which has frequently been bestowed without much historical evidence on such earthworks. In this case, however, fragments of Romano-British pottery have been excavated along with earlier débris; and it does seem reasonable that a military station of some kind should have been set on earlier fortifications to guard the so-called Devil's Highway, which was in fact the Roman road from London to Silchester. The ramparts and ditch can be identified under a palisade of tall beeches on the northern end.

In later centuries there were other military echoes: in the lead-up to the Napoleonic Wars this became the scene of army manoeuvres and mock battles, studied by royalty from high ground above neighbouring Sandhurst.

7D South Hill Park

On the southern outskirts of Bracknell, the park is signposted off A322 roundabout. The fourteen-acre park itself is open all day throughout the year, with a variety of free outdoor weekend entertainments. Its Victorian mansion has become an Arts Centre with studio theatre, cinema, bar and restaurant, art and craft exhibitions, and frequent jazz, folk and classical concerts with varying admission fees.

7E Lily Hill Park

An extensive recreation area lying north of the eastbound A329 from Bracknell towards Ascot, this is reached from a left turn at the roundabout by the Running Horse inn. There is a car-park on the right about half a mile along the curve of Lily Hill Road.

Lily Hill House was built early in the nineteenth century on what is thought to have been the site of an old hunting lodge from the days when this was part of Windsor Forest. Today the building is occupied as business premises, but the grounds are maintained for public use, with a number of picnic areas. A 'tree trail' has been devised through plantations of oak, cedar, fir, pine and many others, labelled to show the varieties which have developed in the parkland here over the years. The waymarked Ramblers' Route mentioned earlier also crosses the park and Longhill Recreation Ground, making its way over B3034, the Forest Road once used by sheep-drovers between London and the West Country.

8 CALIFORNIA COUNTRY PARK, near Wokingham

Take A30 south-west, and on outskirts of Bagshot turn north-west on A322 towards Bracknell. At junction with B3430 turn left on westbound Nine Mile Ride and continue across A321 and across B3016, signposted Arborfield. The entrance to the country park is a short distance along on the right, with a drive leading to two car-parks. This is on the fringe of the Bracknell woodlands dealt with in the preceding entry but is a separate entity under the aegis of Wokingham District Council. Open daily all year round.

Like many of the previously recommended woodlands, this was once part of Windsor Forest. Towards the end of the nineteenth century it was bought by an MP, who enlarged Longmore Lake to its present three-acre size. After the Second World War a developer set up a commercial pleasure park and holiday centre which he dubbed 'California in England', with chalets for three hundred people, a ballroom with a glass floor, miniature railway and zoo. In due course this declined, the ballroom burned down, and today the commercial venture has become a sixty-five-acre park for public use – though along one footpath can still be traced fragments of the miniature railway line.

There are picnic sites, lakeside fishing, a children's play area and a large paddling-pool. Nature trails wind through a nature reserve which takes in woodland, wet heath and bog. A small museum, open during busier times of the year, displays material related to the natural history of the area; and a warden is on duty to answer any questions.

Alternative approach: from M25 junction 15 take westbound M4 towards Reading. At M4 junction 10 follow signs to Wokingham; take southbound A321 towards Sandhurst, then B3016 signposted Finchampstead; and turn right on Nine Mile Ride (as above) signposted Arborfield.

9 STAINES RESERVOIRS

Take eastbound A30 towards Staines. North of Staines, A3044 bisects the reservoirs and offers one of the finest prospects for bird-watchers within the London environs, in spite of the almost uninterrupted roar of fixed-wing fliers on their way into or out of Heathrow. A less busy vantage point can be found via a footpath from B378 along the eastern edge of the reservoirs.

Alternative approach: from M25 junction 14 take southbound A3044 towards Staines, crossing the reservoirs in the opposite direction from the foregoing.

10 THORPE PARK, near Chertsey

Turn towards Staines, then take southbound A320 signposted Chertsey. The park itself is liberally signposted, and there is a special clearly marked spur off roundabout north of Chertsey.

This five-hundred-acre theme and leisure park has been created around extensive lakes re-shaped from gravel diggings, utilizing the expanses of water for water gardens with a bird sanctuary and nature trail, waterbus rides, watersport activities such as surfboarding, water ski-ing and cable water-ski tows, and a ferry to a working farm and shire horse centre. The watersports require pre-booking and payment of an additional fee. Everything else in the park, other than roller-skate hire and some coin-operated amusements, is covered by the entrance fee. This includes children's rides and play areas, pedal boating, a rollercoaster, a cinema, models of famous international structures, a craft centre, British historical displays and a large number of well-placed picnic sites. Picnic lunches can be brought in or bought on site. There is a swimming area, for use only when the weather is clement: lifeguards will be on duty at such times.

Thorpe Farm has been built up around the sort of buildings and agricultural methods one could have expected to see between the First and Second World Wars, to give young people some idea of the pre-supermarket economy. Some of the farm buildings are survivors from the seventeenth century, and the machinery covers many periods leading up to modern scientific tools and usages. The farm animals on show are breeds which were common in the 1930s. There are demonstrations of weaving, pottery and the working of a traditional smithy.

Open daily 10 a.m. from the end of March until the first weekend in September; and from then on, every weekend until early November. Fee. Refreshments in riverboat restaurant, snack bars, and beer and wine shop. WC.

FROM JUNCTION

15

11 BLACK PARK, near Slough

Take westbound M4 towards Slough. At M4 junction 5 take A4 towards Slough and turn north-east on A412 towards Rickmansworth. Left of the road is a westbound minor road signposted Wexham Street, leading to an entrance into a wide parking and picnic area with tables and benches.

A nature trail leads through the grounds, as well as many informal paths. Coarse fishing is allowed free on a lake on which non-powered boats are also permitted: dinghies, canoes and model boats. There are changing huts for swimmers. Refreshment kiosk. WC.

12 LANGLEY PARK, near Slough

Directions as for Black Park (see preceding entry), but Langley Park is on the right of A412 north-east, up Billet Lane, signposted for picnic site 650 yards along on the right.

There is ample space for parking, and near the entrance are benches and tables in a pleasant glade. Beside them begins a specially planted Rotary Jubilee Avenue of World Friendship, sponsored by a number of international Rotarian groups.

Partly landscaped and partly informal parkland, these woods and gardens adapted for public pleasure from a once private estate can be explored adventurously or by well-maintained paths. There are a lake, an arboretum and a farm trail. Seats on what must once have been the terrace of a vanished mansion give a vista of Surrey hills down a long ride. WC.

Alternative approaches to Black Park and Langley Park: at M25 junction 16 turn east on M40 towards London; at M40 junction 1 turn south-west on A412 towards Slough, and parks will be in reverse order from the foregoing.

13 MAIDENHEAD THICKET

Take westbound M4 towards Reading. At M4 junction 9 turn north-west on A423(M) towards Marlow. Crossing A4, there is a car-park entrance on the left immediately beyond the roundabout. Another car-park is set beside a minor road on the right towards Pinkney's Green.

Between them, Maidenhead Thicket and Pinkney's Green offer more than five hundred acres of wide rides, woodland walks and spacious glades for picnicking. In the heart of Maidenhead Thicket is an excavated Belgic farm enclosure known as Robin Hood's Arbour.

NEARBY FEATURE:
Courage Shire Horse Centre. From A4/A423 roundabout take westbound A4 towards Reading. Entrance to the centre is on the left about half a mile along. Displays of shire horses, harness, rosettes and trophies. Enclosure of birds and domestic animals. Children's playground. Picnic areas.

Open 11 a.m.-5 p.m. daily except Monday (unless a Bank Holiday) March to October. Fee (children half-price). Refreshments. WC.

14 THE HOCKETT PICNIC SITE, near Cookham Dean

Take westbound M4 towards Reading. At M4 junction 9 turn north-east on A308(M) and left at Bray Wick roundabout on to northbound A308 through Maidenhead. Continue to junction with A404 and turn left at roundabout onto A404 south-west. The entrance to the parking and picnic site is immediately on the left, giving access to footpaths through Park Wood and the Hockett.

Alternative approach: to avoid Maidenhead town centre, at M4 junction 9 turn north-west on A423(M) and continue past

Maidenhead Thicket on A423 to junction with A404. Turn north-east at roundabout on dual carriageway towards Marlow, and at roundabout junction with A308 continue right round on to south-west-bound dual carriageway, with picnic site immediately on the left, as above.

15 COOKHAM and MAIDENHEAD COMMONS

Take westbound M4 towards Reading. At M4 junction 7 turn north to join A4. At roundabout junction take westbound A4 towards Maidenhead. Immediately across the bridge into the town turn north on A4094, across Widbrook Common to Cookham, then left on B4447 to Cookham Rise and Cookham Dean.

On the right of B4447 out of Cookham there is a large parking space on the meadows, with a footpath to Cock Marsh by the river. There are commonland and riverside walks, many of them taking in scenes familiar from the paintings of Stanley Spencer, especially those close to Cookham bridge. There is a museum with many of his paintings in Cookham village (small fee).

Sumptuous beechwoods north-west of Cookham Dean climb the steep slopes above boathouses and chalets by the shining river, with paths through Quarry Wood and a particularly fine view from Winter Hill. A descending path brings one to Cock Marsh again. Kenneth Grahame lived nearby while writing *The Wind in the Willows*, and it is believed that Quarry Wood may have been the 'wild wood' of the story.

On the other side of the Thames there are long towpath walks in both directions from Marlow's waterfront.

Alternative approach: from M25 junction 16 take westbound M40 towards Oxford. At M40 junction 4 turn south on A404 to Marlow, and right on A4155 into the town. In town centre turn left down High Street and over Marlow Bridge. On south bank take left fork, under A404, make steep climb through Quarry Wood, and so proceed to Cookham Dean.

16 HURLEY

Take westbound M4 towards Reading. At M4 junction 9 turn north-west on A423(M), cross A4 at roundabout on to A423, and cross A404 at next roundabout. Turn left at Hurley Bottom and almost immediately turn sharp right into Hurley village.

There is a large free car-park opposite the church. From here a short footpath leads to the towpath and a footbridge over a narrow channel of the Thames, on to wide grassy islets beside weirs and a marina. On both sides of the bridge there is plenty of space for picnics, for lazing and for watching boats fuss and froth to and fro, taking their turn through the lock.

Alternative approach: from M25 junction 16 take westbound M40 towards Oxford. At M40 junction 4 turn south on A404 past Marlow. Just over a mile past Bisham roundabout turn right for Hurley Bottom and Hurley, as above.

(On this route there is a small picnic site beside A404 at the Hurley Bottom turn-off.)

17 DINTON PASTURES COUNTRY PARK, near Reading

Take westbound M4 towards Reading. At M4 junction 10 take A329(M) north-west towards Reading, then turn off to follow signs to Winnersh. The northbound B3030 past Winnersh station towards Hurst goes past the park entrance on the left.

Entry to this wide expanse of open countryside and lakes bordered by the River Loddon and the Emm brook is free. There are picnic areas, a nature trail and a Country Park Centre in a converted Edwardian farmhouse. In school holidays special activities are organized for children of all ages. Regular monthly bird-watching walks are conducted by the park staff. The lakes offer generous scope for windsurfing, dinghy sailing and canoeing – hire craft and tuition available – and coarse fishing, for which day tickets are sold at the water's edge, season tickets at the park office beside the main car-park.

Open daily all year, dawn to dusk. Refreshments. WC.

18 WELLINGTON COUNTRY PARK, near Reading

Take westbound M4 towards Reading. At M4 junction 11 turn south on A33 towards Basingstoke, and follow signs to Wellington Country Park.

The rural surroundings of a large lake have been developed into a leisure centre of woodland and open space, with picnic areas, five nature trails, a fitness course, a deer park, an enclosure for small animals, and a reconstructed charcoal-burner's camp typical of past trades in this region. The lake offers boating, dinghy sailing and windsurfing. There are radio-controlled model boats, a miniature steam railway and an adventure playground. Various festivals are staged throughout the year, including a craft festival, dog shows, a Shetland pony show and motor rallies. The grounds also house the National Dairy Museum, with an audio-visual programme on the history of dairying.

Open 10 a.m.-5.30 p.m. daily March to October, and winter weekends. Fee. Refreshments. Gift shop. WC.

NEARBY FEATURES:

Stratfield Saye House. Signposted from A33/A32 roundabout which also indicates Wellington Country Park. This elegant seventeenth-century mansion was presented to the first Duke of Wellington in 1817 in gratitude for his final defeat of Napoleon. It contains displays of his personal belongings, his eighteen-ton funeral carriage made from cannon captured at Waterloo, the state coach used at the coronation of Queen Elizabeth II, and part of the National Collection of the British Model Soldier Society. In the grounds are walled gardens, a wildfowl sanctuary and the grave of Copenhagen, the Iron Duke's famous charger.

Open 11.30 a.m.-5 p.m. Easter weekend; Saturdays and Sundays in April; daily (except Friday) May to September. Fee. Refreshments. WC.

Swallowfield Park. North of Wellington Country Park, off B3349. An eighteenth-century reshaping of a seventeenth-century house, with a walled garden of roses, flowering shrubs and trees.

Open 2 p.m.-5 p.m. Wednesday and Thursday, May to September. Fee. WC.

19 HAZELEY HEATH, near Hartley Wintney

Follow route as for Wellington Country Park as in preceding entry, then continue south on A32 and B3011. There are footpaths across the heath and plenty of open space, but only roadside parking. A

minor road from Hazeley, or from the junction south of Wellington
Country Park, leads to Bramshill Plantation, Forestry Commission
woodlands criss-crossed by rides.

20 CHILD BEALE WILDLIFE TRUST, near Pangbourne

Take westbound M4 past Reading towards Newbury. At M4
junction 12 turn west on A4 through Theale. Turn right on A340,
and in Pangbourne turn left on A329 towards Basildon. Entry to the
wildlife park is on the right of the road about two miles west of
Pangbourne.

There are long walks around lakes with wildfowl and flamingos;
spacious pens and field enclosures for pheasants, parrots, owls,
Highland cattle, sheep, llamas, goats and ponies; several picnic
areas, including wide meadows beside the Thames; and river trips
to and from Reading. Close to a children's play and picnic area are
paddling-pools. To add to the colourful displays there is an exotic
ornamental pavilion, statues abound, and a fountain surges and
sparkles above the Three Ponds. The Child Beale Trust also
incorporates the headquarters of the World Pheasant Association,
details of which can be studied at the Information Centre.

Open 10 a.m.-6 p.m. daily except Fridays, April to September.
Fee for car allows free admission to all passengers. Small fee for
individual pedestrians. Refreshments. WC.

NEARBY FEATURE:

Basildon Park (NT). Follow route as for preceding entry.
Entrance to the park is on the left of A329 a short distance past
the Wildlife Trust. There is a small, rough picnic area by the
car-park, but this is liable to be used as an overflow car-park on
busy days. Over four hundred acres of beautiful park, woodland
and garden (which can be visited separately from the house for a
much reduced fee). The mansion itself is an eighteenth-century
house of Bath stone in a classical style. Contents include pictures
and furniture, a room with an incomparable collection of rare
land and sea shells, and 'the Nabob's Room' of Anglo-Indian
furniture and souvenirs.

Open 2 p.m.-6 p.m. Wednesday to Saturday, noon-6 p.m.
Sundays and Bank Holiday Mondays (closed Good Friday),
April to October. Fee. Refreshments. WC.

21 MAPLEDURHAM COUNTRY PARK, near Reading

Take westbound M4 towards Reading. At M4 junction 11 turn north on A33 through centre of Reading and over Caversham bridge. Turn sharp left on A4074. On outskirts of Caversham take minor road to left, signposted Mapledurham.

The riverside picnic park covers a wide sweep of meadows overlooking a broad, frothing weir, in a designated Area of Outstanding Natural Beauty. It is administered by the estate office of Mapledurham House, who charge a small parking fee which is refundable for visitors to the house. The park has limited seasonal opening hours: 10 a.m.-3 p.m. daily during the summer, but with possible further restrictions in a bad summer.

NEARBY FEATURE:

Mapledurham House and watermill. The Elizabethan mansion was built by the Blount family and restored by their descendants. Noted for superb staircases and plasterwork ceilings. The mill is the last working watermill on the Thames, grinding wholemeal flour for sale.

House open 2.30 p.m.-5 p.m. Saturdays, Sundays and public holidays from Easter Sunday until last Sunday in September. Fee. Refreshments. WC.

Mill open noon-5 p.m. same days, plus winter Sundays 2 p.m.-5 p.m. Fee.

Alternative approach: on days when the house is open, there are river trips from Reading right into a private mooring in the grounds of Mapledurham House. These leave from Caversham bridge in Reading, beside which there is a large car-park. (Regular thirty-minute river trips are also made to and from Child Beale Wildlife Trust – see earlier entry.) There is plenty of play and picnic space beside the river in Reading itself, by Caversham bridge and on King's Meadow to the east.

22 WELL PLACE BIRD FARM, Ipsden

Although this is on the extreme limit of our travels, it merits a visit if one has already driven within a few miles of it.

Take westbound M4 past Reading. At M4 junction 12 turn west towards Newbury and at roundabout take northbound A340 to

Pangbourne. Continue north from Pangbourne across toll bridge on B471. At junction with A4074 turn left and then right on minor roads through Ipsden; or follow minor roads through Checkendon and Ipsden.

The bird farm has over a hundred varieties of birds as well as goats, monkeys, donkeys, otters, pet lambs and other animals. There is a picnic site.

Open 10 a.m.-5.30 p.m. daily April to September. Fee (children much reduced fee). Refreshments. Garden centre. WC.

FROM JUNCTION

16

23 BAYHURST WOOD COUNTRY PARK, near Uxbridge
Take eastbound M40 towards London. At M40 junction 1 turn north on A412 towards Rickmansworth. North of the railway line a minor road to the right leads to Bayhurst Wood, about a hundred acres of woodland with paths, bridleways, picnic areas and barbecue sites.

24 BURNHAM BEECHES, near Slough
Take westbound M40 towards Oxford. At M40 junction 2 take southbound A355 towards Slough, and almost immediately turn right on minor road towards Burnham. Several other right turns off A355 lead into Burnham Beeches, and once into the woods there are numerous parking spaces, some formal, some in glades under the trees.

Vast acreages of common and wasteland disappeared during enclosures from Tudor times onwards, and now only a few traces of the medieval landscape of England remain. The five hundred acres of Burnham Beeches represent a rare survivor. Once this was all commonland and scrub used by local people as rough pasture, but by the middle of the nineteenth century such usages had dwindled, while trees had grown up in an undisciplined tangle. Most notable among the beeches are clumps which may well be four hundred years old, warped into strange shapes as a result of being pollarded for fuel. When this custom, too, was abandoned and the trees began to put out new growths, these only added to the grotesqueness of their shapes, and weighed some of them dangerously down.

In 1880 a naturalist rejoicing in the appropriate name of Mr Heath urged that the City of London should take over the area, not just to preserve its character but to provide a recreational facility for the congested, ever-spreading metropolis. The Corporation have administered the region ever since, opening up new roads to make access easier than it had been along the old tracks, but keeping them to a reasonable scale and not cluttering the place up with too many notices and barriers.

In spite of the popularity of 'the Beeches' at weekends, there always seems to be room to picnic and to stroll with little interruption. The agreeable inns nestling among the trees or looking out over a by-road are like remote country hostelries rather than suburban pubs. The Stag Hotel, a rather lumpish Victorian building on the site of an older inn, and Stag Hill remind us of the animals which once frequented these acres. Not far from the Stag is East Burnham House, where Richard Brinsley Sheridan spent his honeymoon after marrying Elizabeth Linley.

Other names of roads and rides strike echoes from the past. Victoria Drive speaks for itself. Mendelssohn's Slope evokes memories of Queen Victoria's favourite composer, who spent a great deal of his leisure time in this grassy vale during his visits to England. Grenville Drive is named after the Lord Grenville who bought a large tract of wasteland at Dropmore and built himself the house which still stands there. He had a sizeable chunk of hill removed so that he could treat himself to an uninterrupted view of Windsor Castle.

NEARBY FEATURE:
Cliveden (NT). Follow signposts through Burnham Beeches towards Bourne End. Entrance gates to Cliveden face the junction of minor roads from Burnham and Taplow. The original seventeenth-century house was for a time rented by Frederick, Prince of Wales, father of George III – which is why the large inn opposite the gates is still called the Feathers. It was in his time

that 'Rule, Britannia' had its first performance, in the turf amphitheatre still existing in the grounds.

Twice burnt down, the mansion was replaced in the middle of the nineteenth century by the existing house, later the home of the Astor family, now a luxury hotel. The extensive grounds are a continuing delight. Lawns, gardens, a shell fountain, a rhododendron valley and a huge, airy terrace lead onto steep cliffside paths down to the bank of the Thames. A sheltered Italian garden became a tranquil cemetery for those who died in the nearby Canadian hospital during the First World War. The water garden is overlooked by a sprightly pagoda, brought here from the Great Exhibition of 1851.

An open-air summer festival, including marionettes and special performances for children, takes place annually.

Grounds open 11 a.m.-6 p.m. or sunset daily, March to December. Fee. Refreshments in the orangery April to October. NT shop. WC.

Alternative approach to Burnham Beeches and Cliveden: from M25 junction 15 take westbound M4 towards Reading. At M4 junction 7 take northern spur to join A4, and at roundabout turn right on eastbound A4. A short distance along, turn left on minor road through Burnham and follow signs to Burnham Beeches.

25 WOOBURN GREEN PICNIC SITE, near Beaconsfield

Take westbound M40 towards Oxford. At M40 junction 2 turn north and then west on A40 along outskirts of Beaconsfield. At western end of the town is a left turn onto southbound B4440, signposted Wooburn Green and signposted for picnic site on the left. Parking space, and tables and benches. This can in fact be incorporated with drives and walks through Burnham Beeches (see preceding entry), since Wooburn Green and Wooburn Common neighbour the Beeches area.

NEARBY FEATURE:

Bekonscot Model Village. Beside Warwick Road in Beaconsfield, lavishly signposted from the centre of the town. Claims to be the oldest model village in the world, with miniature houses, shops, streets, lakes and flowers in a landscaped garden with a model

railway. Includes picnic sites and a shop.
     Open daily 10 a.m. from March to October. Fee.
Refreshments. WC.

26 HAMBLEDEN, near Henley-on-Thames

Take westbound M40 towards Oxford. At M40 junction 4 turn
south on A404 to Marlow. At interchange on outskirts of Marlow
turn westward on A4155 towards Henley-on-Thames. Hambleden
is signposted up northbound minor road at Mill End.

There is a car-park (WC open weekends only) on the left of this
road a short distance from the turn-off, just after a signpost to the
right indicating Rotten Row. From here it is well worth walking
back to the A4155 junction to see Hambleden Mill, a beautiful
weatherboarded complex above a lock, offering one of the most
picturesque sights by the River Thames. It is seen at its best from a
footbridge right across the weir to the far bank.

Past the attractive village inn is another free parking site, from
which a footpath starts across the hillside; and further up the slope
other roadside parking gives access to local footpaths through Ridge
Wood, Henleyhill Wood and other woodlands towards Turville.
The Oxfordshire Way footpath cuts across Turville Heath.

From Hambleden it is only a few minutes' drive into
Henley-on-Thames; or one can reach it by towpath or footpath.
Henley itself has a spacious promenade, riverside greens and
parking and picnic sites open 8 a.m.-8 p.m. on Mill Meadows,
signposted from the western end of Henley bridge. WC.

NEARBY FEATURES:
Stonor House and Park. Reached by minor roads just south of
Turville Heath, or from Henley-on-Thames via A423 north-west
to Assendon and then B480. Occupied by the Stonor family for
eight hundred years, the house has been rebuilt over the centuries
around an original twelfth-century fabric of which some features
still remain. It contains furniture, tapestries, paintings and a
medieval chapel. Extensive deer park overlooked by hillside
gardens, and a prehistoric stone circle restored in the grounds.

     Open 2 p.m.-5.30 p.m. Wednesay, Thursday and Sunday (and
Bank Holiday Monday 11 a.m.-5.30 p.m.) April to September;

also Saturday afternoons in August. Fee (children up to fourteen free, but no more than two children per adult). Picnic site. Refreshments. WC.

Greys Court (NT), Henley-on-Thames. Minor road from Henley to Greys Green. Gabled Elizabethan house with fine plasterwork and chimneypieces. Remnants of an earlier thirteenth-century house include a fortified courtyard with three towers and a keep. A huge donkeywheel is housed in a Tudor wellhouse over a well two hundred feet deep. In the grounds is a tantalizing maze.

Grounds open Monday to Saturday; house Monday, Wednesday and Friday midday-6 p.m. April to September. Fee. Refreshments. WC.

JUNCTIONS
16-21

This region is dominated by the undulating chalk ridge of the Chiltern hills, a sixty-mile section of the limestone belt which stretches from the Dorset coast to the Wash. Although in no way a spectacular mountain range, the escarpment is sometimes so steep that nothing but grass and wiry bushes can get a grip on it. Sudden rises and unexpected gaps provide a chequered panorama of beech woods, bare slopes, rich farmland in the vales, and the occasional splash of colour from a demure, secluded little village tucked away into a tree-shaded cleft.

One of the oldest trackways in England follows the ridge along much of its course – or, rather, a double trackway, since there is both an Upper and a Lower Icknield Way running roughly in parallel. Parts of these have been incorporated in the long-distance route established by the Countryside Commission as the Ridgeway, covering eighty-five miles from Avebury in Wiltshire across part of Oxfordshire and on into Buckinghamshire. There are car-parks at various points along the Way, one commanding fine views from Streatley above Goring, below which several different tracks once converged to ford the Thames. From here the route heads for Whiteleaf Hill and skirts the edge of the Chequers estate before reaching its goal at Ivinghoe Beacon.

These ancient paths are crossed by several of the roads we shall be driving along, and by other more recent tracks: local authorities claim that the Chilterns have fifteen hundred miles of the best maintained footpaths in the country.

Although in the following chapter I have continued with the numerical sequence of M25 junctions, it is possible that a newcomer to the region may prefer to make a first foray from junction 17 to the Chiltern Open Air Museum (see later entry), to get an explanatory preview, as it were, of the whole territory.

KEY

1   West Wycombe Hill
2   Prestwood Picnic Site, Bradenham
3   Home of Rest for Horses, Lacey Green
4   Watlington Hill and Christmas Common
5   Beacon Hill and Aston Wood, near Stokenchurch
6   Chiltern Open Air Museum, near Chalfont St Giles
7   Hodgemoor Wood, near Chalfont St Giles
8   Whielden Gate Picnic Site, near Amersham
9   Ashgrove Picnic Site, near Amersham
10 Chesham Bois Woods, Chesham/Amersham
11 Cockshoots Wood Picnic Site, near Wendover
12 Coombe Hill, near Wendover
13 Whiteleaf Hill Picnic Site, near Princes Risborough
14 Chiltern Forest (Wendover Woods), near Wendover
15 Ashbridge Estate, near Berkhamsted
16 Ivinghoe Beacon
17 Whipsnade Green and Heath
18 Dunstable Downs
19 Quainton Railway Centre, near Aylesbury
20 Stockgrove Country Park, Leighton Buzzard
21 Maulden Wood, near Ampthill

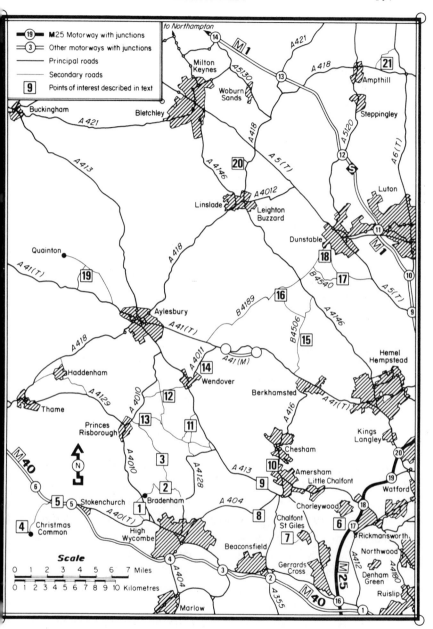

North-West

FROM JUNCTION

16

1 WEST WYCOMBE HILL

Take westbound M40 towards Oxford. At M40 junction 4 turn north-west on A4010 through the outskirts of High Wycombe and then left on westbound A40. Follow signs into West Wycombe.

There is free parking beside a garden centre at the far end of the village, from which one can climb the steep side of Church Hill to St Lawrence's Church and the mausoleum at the top. A less arduous ascent can be made by driving up the winding Church Hill road, past the entrance to West Wycombe Caves, to another free car-park and ample picnic space on the crown of the hill.

Earthworks of a hill fort from the fifth century BC can be identified near the summit, but the most commanding site is that of the church tower topped by a gleaming golden ball within which Sir Francis Dashwood and his friends of the Hell-Fire Club met in the mid-eighteenth century. Their earlier rendezvous had been in Medmenham Abbey, an architectural folly built by the young Dashwood around a ruined monastery a few miles from his home, but it became so notorious and so beset by inquisitive sightseers that the club moved to West Wycombe itself. The ball, into which ten people could be crammed, is still accessible but in recent years has been closed to the public because of vandalism. The interior of the church is copied from the third-century Sun Temple at Palmyra, near Damascus. Masking the body of the church is a stone and flint mausoleum based on Constantine's Arch in Rome, built in 1765 from a legacy willed by one of the club's members, to house the bodies of Dashwood's family and cronies. Niches containing statues of them were later destroyed by puritanical critics of Dashwood's debauchery and supposed devil-worship.

The caves deep within the hillside are thought to be of ancient origin but were much enlarged by Sir Francis when, to give employment to local labourers at a time of economic depression and at the same time provide the Hell-Fire Club with a really private meeting-place, he had material dug out for the construction of a new road between High Wycombe and West Wycombe. This is now overlaid by the straight stretch of the A40 seeming, as one drives westwards, to be heading right into the hill itself below the gilded ball. The catacombs are open to the public, dimly lit but with colourful displays of artificial stalagmites and stalactites, statues and waxworks of Dashwood's friends such as Benjamin Franklin and John Wilkes. It is a great place for children to dodge in and out, pretending to scare one another. At the very far end of the complex, across a narrow stream known as the River Styx, a collection of waxworks representing the Hell-Fire Club is seen settling down to one of its drunken, blasphemous orgies in the Inner Temple.

Caves open 1 p.m.-5 p.m. Saturday and Sunday, November to March; 11 a.m.-6 p.m. Sundays and Bank Holidays, April to October; 1 p.m.-6 p.m. Monday to Saturday in May; 11 a.m.-6 p.m. Monday to Saturday from end of May to first week in September; 1 p.m.-5 p.m. Monday to Saturday, second week in September to end of October. Fee. Café and gift shop. WC.

NEARBY FEATURES:

West Wycombe House and Park (NT). A Palladian mansion built for the first Sir Francis Dashwood and home of the present Sir Francis, premier baronet of Great Britain. The expansive grounds are its finest feature, laid out around a swan-shaped lake on which its creator once sailed a full-rigged ship for the entertainment of his guests, with statuary and classical temples of the Winds and of Apollo – the latter inappropriately used in times past for cock-fighting.

House and grounds open 2 p.m.-6 p.m. Monday to Friday in June; Sunday to Friday in July and August. Closed Good Friday. Grounds only, 2 p.m.-6 p.m. Easter, Spring and May Day Bank Holiday Sunday and Monday. Fee (reduced fee for gardens only). WC.

West Wycombe Motor Museum. A turn-off from minor road towards Bledlow and Chorley leads to museum in eighteenth-century barns at Cockshoot Farm, with changing exhibitions of vintage and veteran cars and bicycles. Special events throughout the season. Video films, and free quiz for children.

Open 2 p.m.-5 p.m. daily July and August; 11 a.m.-6 p.m. Sundays and Bank Holiday Mondays, April to November. Fee. Refreshments. Shop. Picnic site. WC.

2 PRESTWOOD PICNIC SITE, Bradenham

Take westbound M40 towards Oxford. At M40 junction 4 turn north-west on A4010 through outskirts of High Wycombe and then left on westbound A40. At junction on outskirts of West Wycombe turn right on A4010 towards Aylesbury. Turn right on signposted minor road into Bradenham.

The village of red brick and flint has a huge green, almost an informal playing field in itself. Beyond it the road climbing through the woods has several lay-bys which open out onto woodlands honeycombed with footpaths and wooded glades. In his later years at Hughenden Manor, Disraeli learned to love the 'repose in its woods', rightly declaring that a forest was like an ocean – 'monotonous only to the ignorant'.

To reach the larger car-park and picnic site of Prestwood, continue up the slope above Bradenham village and turn right at T-junction signposted Naphill. Continue to next T-junction in the delightful Hughenden Valley, and turn left. Where the road forks by the Harrow inn, take right fork. Immediately beyond the second right turn is Prestwood picnic site on a gentle grassy slope, with benches and tables.

NEARBY FEATURE:

Hughenden Manor (NT). On the slope of a 170-acre estate, this was the home between 1848 and his death in 1881 of Benjamin Disraeli, twice Conservative Prime Minister and later Earl of Beaconsfield. The house was originally a simple Georgian building, but Disraeli's alterations to it have left us with a riot of red brick, with Gothic turrets, pinnacles and other fantasies conceived by E.B. Lamb, since described as a Victorian 'rogue architect'.

The extensive parkland, for which Disraeli himself organized the planting of ornamental trees, and his wife a miniature 'German forest', is open free daily to the public, with parking on the grass. There is also a small picnic site beside the car-park adjoining the house.

House and garden open 2 p.m.-6 p.m. Saturday and Sunday in March; 2 p.m.-6 p.m. Wednesday to Saturday, noon-6 p.m. Sunday and Bank Holiday Mondays, April to October. Fee. Refreshments. WC.

3 HOME OF REST FOR HORSES, Lacey Green-

Follow instructions for Bradenham (see preceding entry). From Bradenham village turn left at top of hill towards Lacey Green. Slad Lane on the right leads to Speen, with a turn-off for Speen Farm and the Home of Rest established in 1886 as a retreat for pensioned-off working horses, moved here in 1971. Ponies, horses and donkeys welcome visitors and can be fed (within reason) with sugar lumps. Open 2 p.m.-4 p.m. daily, except Christmas Day. Small fee. WC.

NEARBY FEATURE:

Lacey Green Mill. This old smock mill, near the crossroads north of Lacey Green, was built in 1650 in Chesham and moved here in 1821. Corn was last ground in it during the First World War.

Open 3 p.m.-6 p.m. Sundays and Bank Holiday Mondays from May to September. Small fee.

4 WATLINGTON HILL and CHRISTMAS COMMON

Take westbound M40 towards Oxford. At M40 junction 6 turn south-west on B4009 to Watlington, then left on minor road to Watlington Hill car-park, on the right of the road. From a distance the 108 acres of chalk down and copse appear as a long, rather crushed hummock, but the seven-hundred-foot height becomes very real as one starts to climb. Flints 'grow' from the chalk here, as Sussex farmers used to complain about their own downlands. There is a natural yew forest, and conditions for walking and picnicking are ideal. In the late eighteenth or early nineteenth century a local eccentric carved the shape of a church steeple in the chalky hillside.

Christmas Common, which runs on from the hill and is served by the same parking space, is thought to have been so called because of a Civil War clash during which Royalists and Parliamentarians contesting the ridge agreed to a brief truce over Christmas 1643 and met here to celebrate.

A minor road north from Christmas Common runs beside Cowleaze Wood, where the Forestry Commission have established a parking and picnic site, and under M40 to Aston Wood (see following entry).

5 BEACON HILL and ASTON WOOD, near Stokenchurch

Follow directions for preceding entry, and immediately after passing under M40 turn left into parking space for Nature Reserve Centre, Beacon Hill and Aston Wood. More than a hundred acres of beech wood on the Chiltern escarpment spread, in fact, both sides of the M40. Footpaths run on through other woods to the north, towards Princes Risborough.

Alternative approach: take westbound M40 towards Oxford; at M40 junction 5 turn north and west on A40, and left and right on minor roads for parking place as above.

FROM JUNCTION

17

6 CHILTERN OPEN AIR MUSEUM, near Chalfont St Giles

Take A412 south to Maple Cross and then follow signpost to 'The Chalfonts'. Entrance to the museum and free car-park is in Newland Park, off Gorelands Lane.

The open-air collection in forty-five acres of parkland has buildings and mementoes representing five hundred years of Chiltern life, with frequent special events, sheepdog trials, craft exhibitions and band concerts. There are a picnic area and a nature trail. This is a good place to start a full-scale exploration of the Chilterns.

Open 2 p.m.-6 p.m. Wednesdays, Sundays and Bank Holidays April to September. Fee. Refreshments. WC.

NEARBY FEATURE:

Milton's Cottage. Half-timbered eighteenth-century 'pretty Box', as one of his students described the cottage in Dean Way where John Milton lived while working on *Paradise Lost* and *Paradise Regained*, first editions of which are included in a display of rare books.

Open 10 a.m.-1 p.m. and 2 p.m.-6 p.m. Tuesday to Saturday, and 2 p.m.-6 p.m. Sunday, February to October; also Spring and Summer Bank Holidays. Fee. Shop.

7 HODGEMOOR WOOD, near Chalfont St Giles

Follow directions as for preceding entry. In Chalfont St Giles turn right by church, and at crossroads near Bottrells Close continue on minor road west. On the left is signposted parking with a picnic area, and paths leading away into the woods.

Alternative approach: from M25 junction 16 take westbound M40 towards Oxford. At M40 junction 2 turn north to roundabout on A40, left on A40 and right on A355 towards Amersham. Turn right on minor road signposted Chalfont St Giles, and turn right into signposted parking and picnic place.

FROM JUNCTION

18

8 WHIELDEN GATE PICNIC SITE, near Amersham

Take A404 westbound to Amersham, and continue on it south of the town towards High Wycombe. After about two miles the picnic site is signposted up minor road to the left, with tables and benches in an attractive, shaded setting below Winchmore Hill. Footpaths lead up the wooded hillside, overlooked by remains of an old windmill.

Alternative approach: from M25 junction 16 take westbound M40 towards Oxford. At M40 junction 3 take northbound A355 through Beaconsfield towards Amersham, turn left on minor road through Coleshill to junction with A404, and turn left towards picnic site signposted a short distance along A404.

9 ASHGROVE PICNIC SITE, near Amersham

Take A404 westwards to Amersham and join A413 north-west towards Wendover. After about two miles there is a minor road to the right signposted for Hyde Heath and picnic site. The parking and picnic areas are happily informal and well served by woodland walks towards Hyde Heath and through Weedonhill Wood.

10 CHESHAM BOIS WOOD, Chesham/Amersham

Take westbound A404 to Amersham and then northbound A416 towards Chesham. The forty acres of beech wood extend from both sides of A416, an oasis between the business and residential spreads of the two towns.

The beech trees are typical of those which once covered so much of the Chilterns, and in summer provide a luxuriant canopy over a carpet of wild flowers and plants. Their preservation is owed mainly to the Woodland Trust, which also administers nearby Tenterden Spinney, a smaller pocket – some five acres – of greenery in the middle of a residential area in Chesham Bois. Both properties are open to local and visiting walkers and strollers.

11 COCKSHOOTS WOOD PICNIC SITE, near Wendover

Take A404 westwards to Amersham and join A413 north-west towards Wendover. 2½ miles beyond Great Missenden the minor road of Cobblers Hill to the left is signposted for parking and picnic site.

Benches are dark and cool – often, to be quite honest, a bit damp – beneath a heavy over-arching of trees. A stile leads from the site into deep woodland. This is decidedly a place for those who want to be well away from the noisy world, and who do not mind negotiating an extremely narrow approach lane with few passing-places.

12 COOMBE HILL, near Wendover

Take A404 westwards to Amersham and join A413 north-west towards Wendover. Slightly less than a mile further on from Cobblers Lane turn-off (see preceding entry) there is a left turn signed Dunsmore. Follow the road through Dunsmore towards Ellesborough, for access to Coombe Hill.

There is quite a stiff climb to the top. At 850 feet it is the highest point of the Chilterns, with the indomitable Icknield Way climbing over it. Sweeping views open up across the Vale of Aylesbury, south-west towards the Berkshire Downs, and far glimpses of the Cotswolds. Robert Louis Stevenson wrote of the great expanse of plain 'variegated near at hand with the quaint pattern of fields, but growing ever more and more indistinct until it becomes a hurly-burly of trees' with, just as today, 'snatches of slanting road'.

Although the hill itself is fundamentally chalk, with slopes clad in elder, whitebeam and juniper, the level patch on its summit is a clay soil bearing only flints, broom, gorse and heather. On this peak stands a monument dedicated to men of Buckinghamshire who died in the Boer War.

13 WHITELEAF HILL PICNIC SITE, near Princes Risborough

Take route as for preceding entry and then continue to B4010 and turn left towards Princes Risborough; or, instead of turning on minor road through Dunsmore, continue on A413 to Wendover, turn left on B4010 towards Princes Risborough, and then proceed as follows. Join A4010 and turn south-west. On outskirts of Princes Risborough turn left up minor road signposted Whiteleaf and Hampden, and signposted for picnic site. The parking and picnic site is set under the trees on the left at the top of the hill.

There is an abundance of open space here, and a choice of footpaths. One leads through beech woods to the top of Whiteleaf Cross, cut into the hillside chalk and visible from far across the vale. It was once thought to have been a prehistoric waymark on the Icknield Way, but later investigation suggests that it was carved out no earlier than the seventeenth century. Walks can be extended along the edge of the golf course, up to the hill fort of Pulpit Hill (once Bullpit Hill, probably the scene of British and Saxon harvest sacrifices and seasonal rites) and down along the edge of the Chequers estate. The redbrick Elizabethan house given by Lord Lee of Fareham during the First World War as a country residence for the Prime Minister of the day can be glimpsed through the trees. Another climb reaches Coombe Hill (see preceding entry).

Alternative approach for this and for Coombe Hill: from M25 junction 16 take westbound M40 towards Oxford. At M40 junction 4 turn north-west on A4010 through outskirts of High Wycombe and continue on A4010 towards Aylesbury. Just through Princes Risborough, turn right on minor road signposted Whiteleaf and Hampden for Whiteleaf picnic site, as above. For Coombe Hill continue on A4010 and then B4010 to turn-off beyond Ellesborough.

14 CHILTERN FOREST (Wendover Woods), near Wendover

Take A404 westwards to Amersham and join A413 north-west towards Wendover. Turn right on A4011 through Wendover. A short distance beyond the town on the right of the road is entrance to the Forestry Commission's Forest District Office, with parking space near their information centre. It is advisable to start from here by obtaining a leaflet which maps walks, trails and resting-places; and for young people keen on woodland orienteering, there is an inexpensive 'Wayfaring Pack' folder, useful not just in the Chiltern Forest but in other Forestry Commission areas in different parts of the country.

The main approach to Wendover Woods themselves is just over half a mile past the Forest District Office, turning sharp right up a minor road signposted St Leonards. Three hundred yards up the slope is an entrance to the woods, with lay-bys beside the well-made road which climbs above a broadening view of the Vale of Aylesbury to a larger car-parking area on a breathtaking summit. There are other parking spaces, the best being perhaps the Cedar Car Park where all the waymarked trails start and finish beside a large information board. One can choose between the varying lengths and times of Daniel's Trudge, Aston Hill Ramble, Bodding Banks, a School Trail and others; and for the faint of heart (or faint of energy) there is a fairly easy-going Introductory Course. When exhausted, either at the prospect or from the result, there are several attractive picnic sites.

Horse trail for permit-holders only.

The concept of recreational 'wayfaring' as established in Wendover Woods and a select number of other English, Scottish and Welsh forest areas is a mixture of pre-planned paths and informal exploration. Instead of sticking to clearly delineated tracks, the visitor is encouraged to go deeper into the woods, at his or her own pace, to enjoy the wildlife and the whole atmosphere of the environment. So that nobody gets hopelessly lost, there are control points at strategic positions, usually drawing attention to some interesting natural feature; but there is plenty of scope for divergence, and with a map one can choose one's own route and one's own level of physical stamina. WC.

FROM JUNCTION
20

15 ASHRIDGE ESTATE, near Berkhamsted

Take northbound A41 past Hemel Hempstead and north-west to Berkhamsted. At north-west end of the town turn right on northbound B4056.

This road runs through a sequence of spacious flinty commons on the Chiltern downland chalk, through woodland and farmland, with parking spaces on both sides and plenty of picnic spaces. A minor road to the west over Aldbury Common also offers ample space for visitors: but the B4506 can boast a greater variety overall.

The estate covers some four thousand acres, encompassing a number of different habitats for trees, plants and animal life. As with so much of the Chilterns, beech woods are its greatest glory, but over recent decades the planned afforestation has included oak, with the aim of maintaining a characteristic English hardwood forest. Birds include wood warblers, woodcock and nightingales. Various species of deer, including muntjak and Chinese deer, have established themselves here, and squirrels are plentiful – and cheeky.

A major car-parking area is to be found west of the road, opposite Ashridge Park. Its entrance is marked by white posts visible from a distance. Inside that entrance is a long avenue of noble trees, interspersed with grassy parking and picnic areas, and at the culmination of the drive is a larger parking space below the Bridgewater Monument. This column was erected in 1832 in memory of the third Duke of Bridgewater, who commissioned the building of England's first major industrial canal from Worsley to Manchester and became known as 'the father of inland navigation'. On payment of a small fee one can climb the 172 steps to the parapet and see for miles around. Close to the foot of the column is a National Trust shop and information centre. Teas are available Saturday and Sunday, and Wednesday to Sunday during school holidays.

Ashridge Park, lying between B4506 and a minor road on the

east from Nettleden, was originally landscaped by 'Capability' Brown, and the gardens around the house were laid out by Humphry Repton. The early-nineteenth-century Gothic Revival mansion is now a management college, but the gardens are open to the public 2 p.m.-6 p.m. Saturday and Sunday, April to October, and visitors are welcome to walk in the grounds but not to picnic. The house is open on certain locally advertised days. Small fee.

NEARBY FEATURES:

Berkhamsted Castle (AM). Large motte and defensive earthworks, probably the work of William the Conqueror's half-brother, with an impressive double moat. Stone walls were added in the twelfth century but were stormed in 1216 by the forces of Prince Louis of France after a two-week siege. The castle was for a time the home of the Black Prince, and remained a favourite royal residence up to the time of Queen Elizabeth I.

Open free of charge daily. Close to Berkhamsted railway station.

Zoological Museum, Akeman Street, Tring. A branch of the Natural History Museum, South Kensington. Mounted specimens of mammals, birds and insects, and a splendid collection of shells.

Open 10 a.m.-5 p.m. Monday to Saturday, Sundays 2.30 p.m.-5 p.m. Closed 24-25 December, New Year's Day, Good Friday and May Day. Admission free. Shop. WC.

16 IVINGHOE BEACON, near Tring

Follow directions as for preceding entry. The Ivinghoe Hills and their crowning Beacon – on which a signal point was set up in Elizabeth I's time to alert the countryside in the event of a Spanish invasion – belong within the compass of Ashridge Estate and can be reached across it by a left turn off B4506 at Ringshall on to minor road over the ridge.

There are several car-parking spaces on the hard-trodden earth of these exposed heights. Here the Ridgeway ends, and other chalky footpaths lead over springy turf pitted with the entrances to rabbit warrens, swooping and climbing to the 756-foot peak of the Beacon. Commanding views over rolling countryside and the levels far below the escarpment include the finely preserved landmark of

Pitstone windmill (see below).

Alternative approach: from M25 junction 20 take northbound A41 to Hemel Hempstead; turn north-west on A4146 towards Leighton Buzzard; and turn left on B489 towards Ivinghoe, with minor road on the left climbing the Beacon.

NEARBY FEATURE:

Pitstone Windmill (NT). About half a mile south of Ivinghoe village, with a path leading to it from B488 south-west towards Tring. One of the post mill's timbers is dated 1627, making it the earliest dated windmill in the country. It was still at work in 1902, but then was damaged in a freak gale and not completely restored until the 1960s.

Open Sundays and Bank Holiday Mondays 2.30 p.m.-6 p.m. May to September. Small fee.

17 WHIPSNADE GREEN and HEATH

Take northbound A41 to Hemel Hempstead and turn north-west on A4146 towards Leighton Buzzard. Turn right on B489 north-east towards Dunstable. Turn right on B4506 towards Ashridge and then left on B4540 signposted Whipsnade Zoo. To the left of the steep climb is the Whipsnade Downs car-park, serving walks up the hillside and open picnic spaces on the ridge towards Dunstable Downs (see below).

This road continues into Whipsnade village, with its huge green and free-ranging heathland beyond, again rich in tracks and informal picnic areas.

Above the village green is the entrance to Whipsnade Tree Cathedral, originally conceived by E.K. Blyth as a memorial to two friends killed in the First World War. Avenues and clumps of trees have been planted to present the appearance of a nave, a cloister walk and chapels in different arboreal styles – a lady chapel, summer chapel and Christmas chapel. There are a gospel oak, a dewpond enclosure and a wealth of glades in which to linger; shadowy copses and ideal hiding-places for children playing through the tree arcades and shrubbery.

NEARBY FEATURE:
Whipsnade Park Zoo. Free parking at top of B4540 on route
recommended above. The five-hundred-acre open-air zoo
displays some two thousand animals and birds in surroundings as
nearly natural as can be achieved in the English climate. Cars may
be driven around much of the area at an additional charge. There
is a zoo train, and a woodland steam railway runs through the
rhinoceros reserve. Children's zoo. Special displays at various
times throughout the year.

Open 10 a.m.-6 p.m. Monday to Saturday; 10 a.m.-7 p.m. or
dusk Sunday and Bank Holiday Monday. Closed Christmas Day.
Fee. Refreshments. Shop. WC.

18 DUNSTABLE DOWNS

The most impressive approach to the Downs is from Whipsnade
(see preceding entry), continuing on B4540 and then left at
Whipsnade Heath crossroads on B4541 towards Dunstable. The
road tips over the crest of the Downs and descends past three
car-parks and picnic areas on the left, the centre one with
refreshment kiosk, information boards and WC.

Walks along the rim of the escarpment offer dizzying views over
the levels below, with Pitstone windmill (see entry for Ivinghoe
Beacon) and the absorbing sight of gliders being winched up and
launched from the airfield at the foot of the slope. The air is often
filled with these silent, graceful gliders, as well as fluttering kites:
wind conditions are ideal for both.

Below the ridge are a number of interesting sites, all within
reasonable walking distance along a network of footpaths. Close to
the road as it approaches the outskirts of Dunstable are the Five
Knolls, a group of round barrows from which both Bronze Age and
Anglo-Saxon relics have been excavated. The skeleton of an early
burial chamber was accompanied by mangled bones of a later age,
suggesting that Anglo-Saxon invaders had for once met their match
in a fight with Romano-Britons doggedly clinging to their
threatened lands.

Another hummock is that of Maiden Bower, an Iron Age camp
beside a disused chalk quarry, reached by footpath from Sewell and
linked by bridleway with Totternhoe Knolls – the earthworks of a

Norman motte-and-bailey castle, now a Nature Reserve with ample parking, a picnic site and a nature trail. For those wanting to drive closer rather than walk all the way, continue downhill on B4541, turn left on B489 and then right on minor road to Sewell and Totternhoe.

NEARBY FEATURE:

Luton Hoo. Reached from Dunstable by A505 and A6129 through Luton, or from M1 junction 10. The house contains Sir Julius Wernher's collections of ivories, Limoges enamels, porcelain and most notably the work of the celebrated Russian goldsmith and jeweller Carl Fabergé. There is also an exhibition tracing Wernher family history related to Luton Hoo, and their records of horse-racing and the history of the horse. The spacious gardens were landscaped by 'Capability' Brown.

Open 11 a.m.-5.45 p.m. Monday, Wednesday, Thursday, Saturday and Good Friday, 2 p.m.-5.45 p.m. Sunday, April to mid-October. Fee (reduced fee for entry to the gardens only). Picnic area. Refreshments. Garden centre. WC.

19 QUAINTON RAILWAY CENTRE, near Aylesbury

Take A41 north-west through Aylesbury. In Waddesdon turn right on minor road to Quainton station. Here is the largest collection of standard-gauge industrial steam locomotives in the country, including many items from the nineteenth century. Display of rolling stock, a small museum, rides on a vintage steam train. In steam 10 a.m.-6 p.m. Sundays and Bank Holidays from Easter to October. Special rallies are held at intervals throughout the year, as announced. Fee variable according to nature of events. Refreshments. WC.

NEARBY FEATURE:

Waddesdon Manor (NT). South of A41 from Quainton. Designed by a French architect in the late nineteenth century in the style of a sixteenth-century château for Baron Ferdinand de Rothschild. Interior famous for its collection of French panelling, furniture, paintings and sculpture. Exhibition of nineteenth-century costume. Gardens laid out by Laine, French landscape artist, making skilful use of sculptures from many parts of Europe to set off the surrounds of trees and shrubs, and two flamboyant fountains. Aviary. Deer park. Children's play area.

Open 2 p.m.-6 p.m. Wednesday to Sunday, late March to late October (grounds 11.30 a.m. Sundays). Good Friday and Bank Holiday Mondays, house and grounds 11 a.m.-6 p.m. Closed Wednesday after a Bank Holiday. Fee (reduced fee for entry to grounds only). Refreshments. Shop. WC.

20 STOCKGROVE COUNTRY PARK, Leighton Buzzard

This and the places following may seem to be some way beyond the planned perimeter of our travels but in reasonable traffic conditions are in fact well within an hour's drive and can be incorporated without much strain into a full day out.

For Stockgrove, take northbound A41 to Hemel Hempstead and then northbound A4146 to Leighton Buzzard. In the town take northbound A418 towards Woburn. Just beyond Heath and Reach is a minor road left to the country park, thirty acres of wood and parkland, with a fishing lake. Open daily throughout the year.

NEARBY FEATURES:

Leighton Buzzard Railway, Pages Park Station, Billington Road. About four miles of narrow-gauge railway, used between 1919 and 1967 for carrying sand from local workings. Steam, petrol and diesel locomotives, including some from Spain and India. Picnic site. Open 11.30 a.m.-4.45 p.m. (3.15 p.m. after October) Sundays, Easter weekend and Bank Holiday Mondays late March to first week in November; and Wednesdays in August. Fee for one-hour trips. Refreshments. Shop. WC.

Woburn Wild Animal Kingdom and Leisure Park, near Woburn Abbey and Deer Park. Safari and leisure complex with collections of lions, tigers, elephants and other species. Boating lakes, amusements centre, pets' corner. Picnic site.

Open daily from 10 a.m. (closing times vary) mid-March to end of October. Fee. Refreshments. Shop. WC.

Alternative approach: from M25 junction 21 take northbound M1. At M1 junction 9 turn north-west on A5 through Dunstable. Turn left on A418 south towards Leighton Buzzard for Stockgrove

Country Park; right on A418 north-east for Woburn Abbey and Woburn Wild Animal Kingdom.

FROM JUNCTION
21

21 MAULDEN WOOD, near Ampthill

Take northbound M1. At M1 junction 10 take northbound A6 through Luton towards Bedford. Twelve miles north of Luton turn left onto large parking and picnic area at entrance to Maulden Wood trails. Only school coaches are allowed to drive through the wood to the coach-park.

This was the first block of woodland in Bedfordshire to be taken over by the Forestry Commission in 1921. The only part of Ampthill Forest with trees old enough to be felled for timber, it is believed to have been in existence since early medieval times. Once there were great oaks here, but most of them disappeared during the First World War, and replanting has concentrated on conifers such as larch, fir and pine.

Paths through the woods give many a sighting of bird life and animals such as squirrels, deer and the occasional fox. Three waymarked walks start from the gate by the picnic area, with informative notes on the various posts: the Rabbit Walk takes about three-quarters of an hour, the Fox an hour, and the Stag an hour and a half, covering different aspects of the area. As well as these forest walks there are two School Trails for the use of organized, authorized parties only.

There is an information centre beside the car-park, with WC here and another one by the Forest Office on the northern edge of the wood.

Ampthill Park, near the town, is a spacious stretch open to the public daily. Some people find a faint air of mystery in certain corners of it; and it was here that the golden hare of the puzzle novel *Masquerade* was buried and ultimately tracked down by a shrewd reader.

NEARBY FEATURES:

Houghton House (AM). On a hill north-east of Ampthill, between A418 and Maulden Wood. This romantic ruin of a seventeenth-century mansion is thought during its heyday to have been the original of 'The House Beautiful' in John Bunyan's *Pilgrim's Progress*, standing on the 'Hill of Difficulty'. Free access daily.

Wrest Park Gardens (AM). Near Silsoe, off A6 south-east of Ampthill. The present house was built between 1834 and 1839 in the French style by the Earl de Grey, whose family had been here for six hundred years. Only a couple of the state rooms are at times open to the public, but the gardens offer a rare visual treat, representing different styles from the beginning of the eighteenth century to the middle of the nineteenth. There are formal canals, an artificial lake, a Chinese bridge and attractive follies such as a classical temple and a rustic ruin. The Great Garden, with the Long Water as its axis, was laid out between 1706 and 1740 by the then Duke of Kent; and, inevitably, 'Capability' Brown had a hand in some of the other features.

Open 9.30 a.m.-6.30 p.m. Saturday, Sunday and Bank Holidays April to September. Small fee. Refreshments. WC.

JUNCTIONS

20-27

In this northerly direction it is harder than in most of the others to tell where London leaves off and other conurbations begin. Suburban spread, 'garden cities', light industry functioning or abandoned, and swathes of motorways occupy a large part of the countryside, leaving very little unspoilt space for leisure. Or so it may seem at first glancing at the map. One needs to look, as it were, between the trunk roads and the encroaching houses, factories and scrap heaps for a space in which to breathe. The M25 itself goes largely through built-up areas here (and in a couple of cases right underneath them) in complete contrast to the open downlands and wide vistas of its southern arc.

Nevertheless, there are compensations. The existence of three other motorways heading north, virtually parallel for the earlier parts of their route and then gradually fanning out, makes it possible to travel further and faster: one can, for example, from the M25/M11 interchange be in Cambridge within three-quarters of an hour without exceeding the speed limit. Although this book has been deliberately restricted to a choice of sites within easy range and does not deal with cities and major towns, in this chapter a few slightly more distant ventures are suggested towards the end of some sub-sections. All, no matter how scattered they may appear on a map, are easily attainable.

KEY

1. The Ver-Colne Walk
2. Whippendell Wood Forest Park, near Watford
3. Aldenham Country Park, near Elstree
4. Verulamium, St Albans
5. Symondshyde Great Wood, near Hatfield
6. Sherrards Park Great Wood, Welwyn Garden City
7. Ayot Greenway, near Welwyn
8. Knebworth Country Park, near Stevenage
9. Fairlands Valley Park, Stevenage
10. Rowney Warren, near Shefford
11. Trent Park Country Park, near Enfield
12. Whitewebbs Park, Enfield
13. Lee Valley Regional Park
14. Baas Hill Common, near Broxbourne
15. Bencroft Wood, near Broxbourne
16. Wormley Wood, near Broxbourne
17. Broxbourne Wood, near Broxbourne
18. Broxbourne Woods bridleways and trails
19. Hoddesdon Park Wood, near Hoddesdon
20. Great Wood Country Park, Northaw
21. Cole Green Way, near Hertford
22. Waltham Abbey
23. Epping Forest

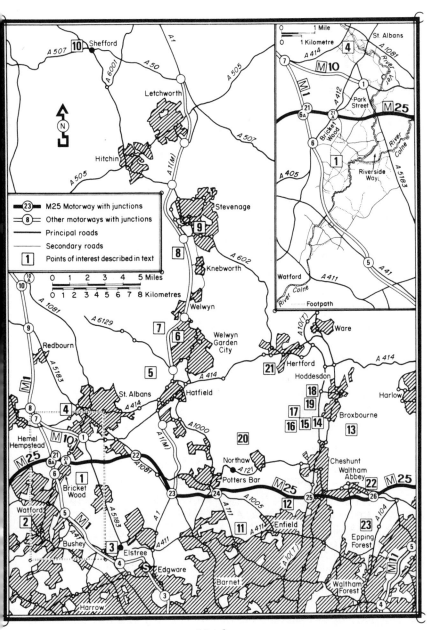

North

1 THE VER-COLNE VALLEY WALK

This extended country park can be picked up at various points along a route between Watford and St Albans, most of them close to the rivers Colne and Ver. From M25 junctions 17, 18, 19 and 20 follow signs to the southern fringes of Watford, where the real beginning of the waymarked walk is to be found off A412 south of the Watford-Rickmansworth railway line, where Watford Linear Park is being developed along the Colne. There are views through the impressive arches of the railway viaduct towards Bushey. Footpaths spread out from the river bank, and soon one is within easy walking distance of Watford Museum in the restored eighteenth-century mansion of Benskins Brewery.

North-east of the town, Bricket Wood Common – signposted off A405 between Watford and St Albans near the M25/M1 interchange – is incorporated in the route: a wetland heath which has been designated a Site of Special Scientific Interest. An informal recreation and picnic area known as Riverside Way has been established beside old gravel pits near Colney Street, with safe paddling for children, paths for riders and walkers, and pleasant prospects along the river valley. This can be reached from Bricket Wood by a minor road joining A5183 near Radlett and turning north to a parking space in Drop Lane, left of the main road. Alternative approaches to this are via B462 from Watford to Radlett and then turning north on A5183; or from M25 junction 21A via M10 junction 1 to southbound A5183 towards Radlett.

Beside the walk is Moor Mill, a watermill thought to be more than five hundred years old, powered by the River Ver and producing flour until shortly before the First World War. A later brick-built watermill, Park Mill, on the eastern side of A5183 near Radlett's disused aerodrome, was also worked by a diversion of the Ver until the middle of that war. There is plenty of scope for picnics nearby on Park Street open space, near Park Street railway station.

On the walk just south of St Albans, near the golf course, are

Sopwell Ruins, the jagged remnants of a house built in the sixteenth century from stones of a dismantled nunnery. Beside the old railway line a footpath across the golf course follows the track of a Roman road, just one of several in the neighbourhood of the great historic settlement at the end of the Ver-Colne walk (see later entry for Verulamium).

2 WHIPPENDELL WOOD FOREST PARK, near Watford

Take southbound A41 and A411 towards Watford. In the outskirts of the town turn right on minor road signposted 'The Langleys', past the impressive bulk of converted Grove Mill beside the course of the River Gade and the Grand Union Canal. At a corner of woodland is a car-park signposted Whippendell Wood Forest Park.

Beside this large parking space in a delightful wooded glade is a picnic site with benches and tables, and an abundance of massive tree stumps and fallen trunks to perch on, scramble over or hide behind. Wide paths lead off into the woodland. A public footpath skirting the West Herts Golf Club joins an ornamental stone bridge across the canal through Cassiobury Park, itself one of the most luxuriant areas of parkland in the region.

Cassiobury Park, open daily all year round, can also be reached from the centre of Watford, past the hospital and via Rickmansworth Road and Parkside Drive, through imposing entrance gates once guarding the estate of the Earls of Essex.

In Nascot Wood Road, on the eastern side of the Hemel Hempstead road out of Watford, are Cheslyn Gardens, with a fine spread of flowers and plants together with an aviary, woodland walks and an ornamental water garden. Open daily except Thursday, 10 a.m.-5 p.m. May to September, 10 a.m.-4 p.m. the rest of the year.

FROM JUNCTION

21

3 ALDENHAM COUNTRY PARK, near Elstree

Take southbound M1, and at M1 junction 5 turn onto southbound A41 towards London. Near Elstree turn left and follow signposts to country park.

The park provides a large expanse of woodland, meadowland and open water, with picnic benches and tables close to the car-park and the lake. There are other formal picnic areas as well as shaded glades for informal picnics and recreation. Several miles of walks and trails include a nature trail, a path around the lake, and one across the dam. Within an area specially designed for children are an adventure playground and a pets' corner.

The lake was once a reservoir, dug by French prisoners of war during the Napoleonic Wars, to maintain the river levels after the cutting of the Grand Union Canal. Now it has a sailing club and, for the benefit of the general public, a launching point to which one's own boat can be brought on Tuesday and Thursday evenings from May to September. Day or season tickets are available for fishing from June to March, and fishing punts can be hired.

New woodland is being developed to enhance the already attractive appearance of the whole area. A double avenue of oaks offers a view of Aldenham House, home in the nineteenth century of the first Lord Aldenham.

An information kiosk has plans and leaflets of the park, news of special events during the summer months, and details of guided walks at certain times throughout the year.

Visitors are asked not to feed the resident animals at random but at specified times may offer them food bought from the staff, under supervision of a park ranger. These animals include longhorn cattle, rabbits, some very sociable goats and various breeds of fowl.

Open 9 a.m.-8 p.m. or dusk daily (10 a.m. on Mondays). WC.

Alternative approach: from M25 junction 23 take southbound A1 towards London, and right on A411 westbound through Elstree, following signs to country park.

4 VERULAMIUM, St Albans

At the time of going to press, feeder roads and exits for junctions 19-23 have not been completed, and it is possible to give only a general guide on the basis of information currently available. It should be possible to approach St Albans with almost equal ease from junctions 19, 21A and 22, but the route to Verulamium avoiding the town centre is the one recommended here.

From junction 21A with A405 take B4630 (once the A412) signposted Chiswell Green. On the outskirts of St Albans follow signposts to Roman Verulamium, where the Ver-Colne Valley Walk (see earlier entry) ends. Behind the museum is a large car-park, with a minimal charge for a full day.

Admission to the wide expanses of parkland is free. The River Ver runs through the grounds, and there is a large lake whose ducks are always delighted to be friendly provided enough crumbs are forthcoming: they can detect the rustle of a paper bag from many yards away. As well as the lake there are a children's paddling-pool and a model boat pond.

The important Romano-British settlement of Verulamium was the only place in Britain to be granted the status of a *municipium*, whose inhabitants had privileges almost equal to those of full Roman citizens. The original Belgic tribal capital was in Prae Wood, now on the other side of the modern A414, in later centuries an oak and hornbeam coppice but now largely coniferous. The Romans shifted the tribal centre to this new, grandiose setting. Sections of stone wall, towers, a hypocaust and a mosaic floor remain, with other archaeological finds on display in the museum. The hypocaust and floor are sheltered in a small brick building in the middle of the park. Immediately across the A414 from the museum is a huge open-air theatre, with its own car-park.

Grebe House Wildlife Centre – admission free – within the main grounds has a small garden in whose constricted space has been laid out a living exhibition of woodland, downland and pond habitats characteristic of the region. From the centre a nature trail leads over the fields and between trees planted in more recent times, after the Roman city had been excavated and the park established by soil dumping and seeding to raise the level of the water meadows. There is an instructive grouping of maple, sycamore, pine, hawthorn, oak and chestnut, and a carefully devised cluster of decorative trees beside the hypocaust building.

Park open daily, free. Museum and hypocaust (fees) open 10 a.m.-5.30 p.m. weekdays, 2 p.m.-5.30 p.m. Sunday, April to October; 10 a.m-4 p.m. weekdays, 2 p.m.-4 p.m. Sunday, November to March. Theatre (fee) open weekdays 10 a.m.-5 p.m., Sunday 2 p.m.-5 p.m. Refreshment kiosk in park. WC.

NEARBY FEATURES:

Gardens of the Rose, Chiswell Green. Showground and collection of thirty thousand roses, administered by the Royal National Rose Society. Trial grounds and display of new varieties.

Open 9 a.m.-5 p.m. weekdays, 10 a.m.-6 p.m. Sunday, June to end of September. Fee (accompanied children under sixteen free). Refreshments. Free car-park. WC.

Kingsbury Watermill Museum. Sixteenth-century mill on River Ver, on the edge of Verulamium. Working waterwheel and collection of old farm implements.

Open 10.30 a.m.-6 p.m. Tuesday to Saturday, noon-6 p.m. Sunday, March to November; 11 a.m.-5 p.m. Tuesday to Saturday, noon-5 p.m. Sunday, December to February. Closed 25 December to January. Small fee. Refreshments. WC.

FROM JUNCTION

23

5 SYMONDSHYDE GREAT WOOD, near Hatfield

Take northbound A1(M) and A1. From ring road around Hatfield take minor road westwards off roundabout past Hatfield aerodrome, through Hatfield Garden Village to car park in Hammond's Lane. Beside the car-park is a picnic area with tables and benches, and there are seats at intervals along a 550-yard trail, almost the first half of which is negotiable by wheelchairs: where it gets more difficult, a seat and turning-point are provided.

This nature trail is waymarked with fifteen points of special interest, drawing attention to the range of wildlife habitats. Starting from the heath and grassland near the car-park, the track passes recent growths of birch but leads on through a mainly oak and hornbeam coppice. There are open spaces where heather is being encouraged to grow again by the local countryside management service after being virtually extinguished in the shade of neighbouring trees, a number of which have been removed. Some hollows in the more open ground are probably the remains of old gravel pits.

Towards the end of the nature trail is a relic of the once busy trade of charcoal-burning. This consists of a portable metal kiln with a hole in its removable lid for a chimney. After adjacent oaks had been coppiced – that is, cut down to ground level at intervals of up to twenty years to provide poles and stakes for fencing and fuel – the wood was burned in the kiln to evaporate the water content, tars and resins, leaving after a couple of days a residue of solid black charcoal.

NEARBY FEATURE:

Hatfield House. Entrance from A1000 immediately opposite Hatfield railway station. Well signposted from the town centre and from surrounding roads. Jacobean mansion with relics and famous portraits of Queen Elizabeth I, tapestries and armour. Exhibition of fashion through the ages, and collections of model soldiers and motor vehicles. The original palace in which young Bess spent a formative part of her childhood stands in the gardens, and stages Tudor banquets several evenings a week throughout the year.

Open noon-5 p.m. Tuesday to Saturday, 2 p.m.-5.30 p.m. Sundays, 11 a.m.-5 p.m. Bank Holiday Mondays, late March to middle of October. (Closed Good Friday.) Fee. Refreshments. Shop. WC.

6 SHERRARDS PARK GREAT WOOD, Welwyn Garden City

Take northbound A1(M) and A1. At junction north of Hatfield
where motorway renews, turn onto northbound B197. Access to
the park is to be found on the right of this road, by minor road into
Welwyn Garden City. There are 180 acres of wooded walks,
including part of an old railway line which continues on the far side
of A1(M) to the west as the Ayot Greenway (see following entry).

7 AYOT GREENWAY, near Welwyn

Take northbound A1(M) and A1. At junction north of Hatfield
where motorway renews, turn on to northbound B197. Opposite
Sherrards Park Great Wood (see preceding entry) turn left onto
westbound minor road to Ayot Green, and turn right at fork
immediately over the motorway.

Ayot Greenway can be picked up at various points along its
route, most easily between Ayot Green and Ayot St Peter, at
Sparrowhall bridge, and close to its western end at Blackbridge
gravel pit on the outskirts of Wheathampstead. Also at Wheathampstead, a short distance south of the River Lea, are the Devil's
Dyke and the Slad, great earthworks and gulleys now tranquil
under over-arching trees but once, it is believed, the site of the tribal
capital of Cassivellaunus which Julius Caesar attacked and
subjugated in his invasion of 54 BC.

The route of the Greenway follows a section of abandoned
railway line which once linked Welwyn, Luton and Dunstable. In
its day this branch line was of considerable importance to local
trade and industry, and the walker along its $2\frac{1}{2}$ miles through
tree-lined cuttings and then up its gentle climb above the rolling
countryside is treading at a leisurely pace over a once busy, essential
lifeline for local communities. The hat industry and then the later
motor industry of Luton employed its services: at one period
Vauxhall cars were providing two forty-waggon trainloads every
day. Chemicals and gravel travelled along the line; both workmen
and their materials were brought in during the construction of
Welwyn Garden City in the 1920s; and local nurseries were
supplied by rail with consignments of manure from London Zoo.
Passenger traffic was of less consequence, but the branch did have a
few distinguished patrons: George Bernard Shaw used it regularly

during his years at Ayot St Lawrence.

Even before the 'Beeching axe' fell upon it, the line was fading in significance and was certainly not helped by the utter destruction of Ayot station in 1948 by a stray spark from a steam locomotive. The heat of the blaze was such that the rails through the station were buckled. Later, regular steam services were abandoned, and all passenger traffic ceased in 1965.

When the county council set about establishing this country walk, it was realized that the rickety Blackbridge near the gravel pits was unsafe, so a unit of the SAS was encouraged to carry out a training exercise during which it was blown up. Today a bridleway is carried over the line by ramps.

Railway embankments have always provided rich habitats for a wide variety of flora and fauna. Here the wild flowers include rose and willow herb, and among the trees and shrubs are hawthorn, blackthorn, willow, broom, oak, ash, hornbeam and birch. Butterflies and birds such as tits, finches and warblers flit in and out, and in the shelter of the cuttings on a summer's day there is usually a lazy, soothing droning and rustling, very good for the nerves after a spell on that modern substitute for the old railway lines – the motorway.

NEARBY FEATURE:

Shaw's Corner, Ayot St Lawrence (NT). The home of George Bernard Shaw from 1906 until his death in 1950, with several of the rooms maintained exactly as in his lifetime.

Open 2 p.m.-6 p.m. Monday to Thursday, Sunday and Bank Holiday Monday noon-6 p.m., April to October. Closed Good Friday. Fee.

8 KNEBWORTH COUNTRY PARK, near Stevenage

Take northbound A1(M) and A1 towards Stevenage. At Stevenage South interchange there is signposted direct access to the park.

The estate has been the home of the Lytton family since the late fifteenth century. In the nineteenth century their Tudor mansion was lavishly converted into a Gothic fantasy, complete with battlements, pinnacles, heraldic devices and gargoyles, by the novelist and politician Edward Bulwer-Lytton, once a popular best-seller with romances such as *Rienzi* and *The Last Days of Pompeii*. It was as an MP that he first met and soon became friends with Charles Dickens, at the time reporting on parliamentary debates. Dickens and Wilkie Collins were frequently entertained at Knebworth, Dickens produced plays there, and some of his letters are displayed in the study.

A later Lord Lytton became Viceroy of India, and there is a British Raj exhibition and audio-visual display commemorating the great Delhi Durbar of 1877.

As well as transforming the house, the novelist turned the original Tudor orchard into a showy Victorian garden. Early this century its layout was simplified by Sir Edwin Lutyens, and a herb garden designed by Gertrude Jekyll was introduced. There are walks through 150 acres of parkland, including a well-devised nature trail, together with an adventure playground, picnic areas and a narrow-gauge railway.

House open noon-5 p.m. Sundays, Bank Holidays and school holidays April to May, then daily until mid-September except Mondays. Park open 11 a.m.-5.30 p.m. same days. Fee (reduced fee for park only). Refreshments. Shop. WC.

9 FAIRLANDS VALLEY PARK, Stevenage

Take northbound A1(M) and A1 towards Stevenage. At Stevenage South interchange turn east to roundabout junction with A602; turn left into the town; and at next roundabout turn right for Six Hills Way and entrance to large public park, open daily. The name of the road derives from a line of six round barrows within the park – not prehistoric in origin, like so many such mounds, but actually marking the site of Roman burials.

10 ROWNEY WARREN, near Shefford

Take A1(M) and A1 past Letchworth. Turn left on westbound A507 to Shefford, and north-west on A600. Just past AA telephone box on the left turn into Sand Lane, which leads to car-park and picnic area on the left.

The warren consists of 280 acres of mainly coniferous woodland, though there are some staunch oaks surviving from the original plantations of the middle nineteenth century. In 1972 a group of schoolgirls studying biology at the Robert Bloomfield School in Shefford laid out a nature trail so effectively that the Forestry Commission encouraged them to expand it for the use of other schools and visitors.

There are fifteen trail posts to guide the walker through plantations of pine, larch and the occasional oak. Some of the trees have nesting boxes for birds. Several types of fern, lichen and moss flourish, and the keen observer may be able at intervals to identify tracks of fox, squirrel and badger. The hollows of two old ironstone quarries are now softened by a coating of plants, and sand martins frequent the holes in their sides.

FROM JUNCTION
24

11 TRENT PARK COUNTRY PARK, near Enfield

Take southbound A111. About two miles along this road across Enfield Chase is an entry on the left to parking and picnic area; and another parking space can be found beside an eastbound minor road from Ferny Hill towards Enfield.

Here there are about 680 acres of wood, parkland and gardens with picnic areas, a lake, fishing and golf. A nature trail and bridleways have been laid out through the woodlands, with a special walk for the visually handicapped. On the fringe of the park, just south of the minor road referred to above, is an obelisk erected by Sir Philip Sassoon in memory of the first Duke of Kent, father of Queen Victoria.

Open daily. Refreshments. WC.

On the other side of A111 begins the two-mile stretch of Monken Hadley Common, ancient woodland which was once part of the extensive Enfield Chase forest.

NEARBY FEATURE:
Forty Hall, on Forty Hill, Enfield, west of A10. The early

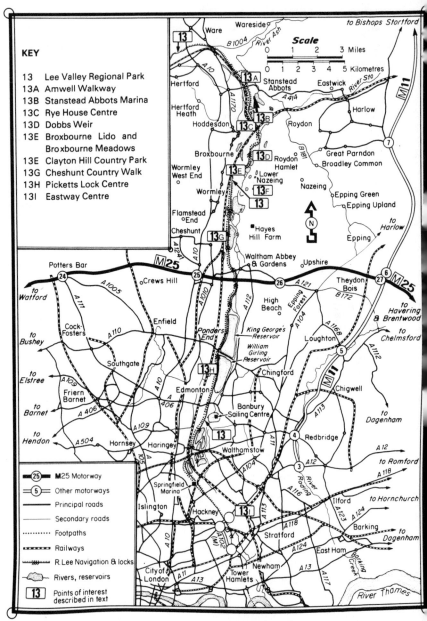

KEY

13   Lee Valley Regional Park
13A   Amwell Walkway
13B   Stanstead Abbots Marina
13C   Rye House Centre
13D   Dobbs Weir
13E   Broxbourne Lido and
       Broxbourne Meadows
13E   Clayton Hill Country Park
13G   Cheshunt Country Walk
13H   Picketts Lock Centre
13I   Eastway Centre

Lee Valley Regional Park

seventeenth-century mansion of the then Lord Mayor of London, with modifications in the following century, including fine plaster ceilings. Displays of furnishing and paintings, and regular temporary exhibitions. Picnic site in grounds.

Open 10 a.m.-6 p.m. Tuesday to Friday (5 p.m. October to Easter); 10 a.m.-8 p.m. Saturday and Sunday (5 p.m. October to Easter). Admission free. Refreshments. WC.

FROM JUNCTION

25

12 WHITEWEBBS PARK, Enfield
Take southbound A10 and at first roundabout turn right on westbound minor road through Bulls Cross. There is parking space on the left for the parkland footpaths of Whitewebbs Park.

NEARBY FEATURE:
Forty Hall. See preceding entry.

13 LEE VALLEY REGIONAL PARK
Take northbound A10. North of Cheshunt turn on northbound A1170 through Broxbourne. Follow signposts on eastbound roads to various riverside features.

This approach is in fact only one of several to access points for the Lee Valley complex, less a park than a succession of differing sites for a range of outdoor and indoor activities – walking, riding, sailing, cycling, day trips on the river, swimming and ice skating.

Early in the seventeenth century the New River was cut to provide London with water, and during the time of the Great Plague it was used by watermen to carry food and other supplies into the stricken City. During the next century the River Lea (or Lee) from Ware into the East End of London was made a lot easier for commercial barge traffic by the digging of a new canal section and adaptation of the existing waterways to create the Lea

Navigation. Its business uses dwindled after the Second World War; but in 1966 the Lee Valley Regional Park Authority was established to clean up the banks and meadows and maintain leisure facilities without imposing too rigid a pattern on the natural surroundings.

The simplest way to summarize the amenities currently available is to follow the course of the river and navigation from north to south. In general these selected sites are accessible via spurs east of A10 between Ware and Hackney, and east of A1170 from Ware to Cheshunt, and from A1010 towards Tottenham.

On certain Sunday afternoons in spring and summer there are conducted nature walks from a number of venues: details are available from local information offices or from the Lee Valley Association, 628 High Road, London N17.

13A Amwell Walkway

This track follows the course of an abandoned railway branch line to Buntingford, through Easney Woods, and can be picked up from Ware along the southbound Lee Navigation towpath, or northwards along the towpath from Stanstead Abbotts. This is a favourite haunt of bird-watchers: as well as ducks and waders in the silt lagoon there are rarer species such as the osprey, great grey shrike and hawfinch.

At Great Amwell village is Van Hages Garden Centre and Mini Farm, open daily 9 a.m.-6 p.m. (farm closing 5 p.m.). A miniature railway operates 9 a.m.-5 p.m. on Sundays. WC.

13B Stanstead Abbotts Marina

A base for cruising on the rivers Lee and Stort, with facilities for mooring and repairs.

13C Rye House Centre

Only the brick gatehouse remains of the building in which the Rye House Plot to murder Charles II and James, Duke of York, was hatched in 1683 by a group of disillusioned Whigs – for which they, and not the royal brothers, paid with their lives. Today it is no more than a picturesque adjunct to the parking and picnic sites, riverside meadows, boat-hire facilities and Rye House Nature Reserve. Open 10 a.m.-4 p.m. Saturdays and Sundays, this reserve is cared for by the Royal Society for the Protection of Birds, who have an information centre and bird-watchers' hide here. It is also possible to obtain permits for weekend bird-watching on the nearby lagoons of the Thames Water Authority.

13D Dobbs Weir

Little more than five minutes' drive from Rye House (see above), this area includes a caravan park off Essex Road, reached from the A1170 through Hoddesdon. Beside it are expanses of landscaped water meadows sloping gently down to the river, offering small boat launching facilities and day-ticket fishing, with special arrangements for disabled anglers.

Picnic sites and towpath walks complete the picture. One footpath leads a short distance to Admirals Walk Lake, one of the many gravel pits in the neighbourhood which are alive with wintering duck.

The caravan site is open from the Sunday before Easter until the end of October.

13E Broxbourne Lido and Broxbourne Meadows

These are signposted at the traffic lights on A1170 through the centre of Broxbourne and, again, further along the eastbound minor road towards the water's edge.

The Lido has an indoor heated swimming pool with a wave-maker, tropical plants, sauna, solarium and riverside sunbathing terraces. Holiday chalets can be hired by the week or for a short break.

Old Mill Meadows are reached from a right turn off the Lido road, following an attractive stretch of the New River crossed by neat little bridges which look as if they had been assembled from a modellers' kit. Past the church there is a left turn down a steep, narrow hill to a beautifully situated waterside car-park. Beyond it, along the banks, are large picnic and play areas, with an abundance of tables and benches, and woodland walks. Holiday chalets are available here also, and there are waterbus trips on summer Sundays and Bank Holidays, and boats for hire for an hour or two, or for extensive longboat journeys, linking up with the Regent's Canal and the Grand Union Canal. Again there is a fine flourish of little bridges, and every now and then the viaduct slung low above the

water resounds to the roar of a fast train.
  Information centre. Refreshment kiosk. WC.

13F Clayton Hill Country Park

These thirty acres of open parkland are to be found south of
eastbound B194 from A1170 towards Lower Nazeing. The views
are surprisingly open and refreshing, somehow undominated by
local housing and the urban sprawl of its near neighbours. There is a
placid lake with an island croaking and cackling with wildlife, and
plenty of tables and benches for picnics.

13G Cheshunt Country Walk

There are two ways of reaching these meadows: either from the
parking space near Cheshunt railway station or from the B194
north of Waltham Abbey. From a large picnic site with tables and
benches there are walks across the meadows and beside the
reservoir. A permit is necessary for coarse fishing from the bank of
the reservoir.
  At Turnford and Fishers Green, old pits now provide a home for
owls, finches, warblers, thrushes, wagtails and many breeds of duck.
Cormorants are regular winter visitors.

13H Picketts Lock Centre

This is well signposted from roads running parallel with the Lee
river and park between Enfield and Edmonton, and from the
roundabout junction of the North Circular Road (A406) and A10.
  Open daily throughout the year, the leisure centre offers a
bewildering choice of activities for visitors, including bowls, a
putting green, a nine-hole golf course, tennis and football. Under
cover are a swimming pool, with supervised lessons for under-fives,
a sauna, a solarium and roller skating. Helpfully there is a crèche,
open on weekdays, where children between 2½ and five years of age
can be left under qualified supervision. Refreshments. WC.
  Plenty of towpath walking in both directions. A path beside the
Girling Reservoir to the north continues past King George's
Reservoir, where there is sailing for club members only. A
southbound path leads to Banbury Sailing Centre and to Springfield
Marina.

131 Eastway Centre

Here we are getting well into London. The sports and leisure centre, situated off Quarter Mile Lane, Leyton, has forty acres of landscaped parkland with picnic sites and walks, a caravan park and camp site, and the Eastway Cycle Circuit with equipment available for hire. Sporting activities also include squash, badminton, netball, tennis and football, with free changing and shower facilities. Refreshments. WC.

14 BAAS HILL COMMON, near Broxbourne

Take northbound A10. North of Cheshunt turn on northbound A1170 towards Broxbourne. In Broxbourne turn left at roundabout on minor road signposted Broxbourne Woods. To the immediate left of the bridge over the A10 is a large parking area on Baas Hill Common with picnic tables and benches, and plenty of open space.

15 BENCROFT WOOD, near Broxbourne

Take northbound A10 and follow directions to Baas Hill Common as in preceding entry. Continue westwards from the common along White Stubbs Lane. On the left are two car-parks, east and west, for Bencroft Wood – very poorly marked, so that it is all too easy to shoot past.

It has been fairly well established that the wood dates back several hundred years. Hornbeams had already been planted here when the wood was shown on a 1766 map. A hard wood thriving on heavy clay soil, this was much used for tool handles and as firewood, coppiced on a rotation of about ten years. All this came to an end about forty years ago. Modern management of the site after a long period of neglect has led to a thinning of much of the tangle which had choked the area, now allowing a greater variety of vegetation below the trees and establishing habitats for wildlife.

As well as opportunities for unhurried strolling there are two waymarked trails, one starting from each car-park, and a route specially maintained for horse riders. Each marked walk takes in about half of the woodland, with a mixture of birch, hornbeam coppice and bracken; and both are designed to skirt the southern rim of the wood with its views across placid, open farmland. Those with time and energy to spare can switch from one route to the other where they converge near two ponds in the heart of the wood.

Frequent guided walks through the Hertfordshire countryside are advertised when appropriate on the noticeboards in both car-parks.

The western parking space is also a good base for walks through Wormley Wood (see following entry).

16 WORMLEY WOOD, near Broxbourne

Follow directions as for preceding entry and use Bencroft Wood western car park.

Wormley Wood is a 340-acre Site of Special Scientific Interest, running on south-west from Bencroft Wood and rather hard to distinguish from it. Almost entirely ancient, this is the largest oak-hornbeam wood in the country still in its semi-natural state. Wild in appearance, it can nevertheless be explored by footpaths almost as erratic as the streams and gulleys which twist through it. The range of mosses found within the woodland is unique, and wildlife species include bats and all three types of British woodpecker.

Beside the eastern boundary of Wormley Wood is the twelve-acre Nut Wood, of quite a different character from its neighbour. Little has been done to it over the last thirty years, and it is now dense with birch, hazel, oak and hornbeam coppice, and carpeted with tangled ferns. The nearest car-parking space is, as for Wormley Wood, in Bencroft Wood.

NEARBY FEATURE:

On the northern side of White Stubbs Lane, just before reaching Bencroft Wood from Baas Hill Common, is Paradise Park, opened to the public in August 1985. Once Broxbourne Zoo, this has been rebuilt completely and brought up to modern wildlife park standards, and will be expanded over coming years. There is a large deer park, and in the zoo enclosures are Vietnamese pot-bellied pigs, llamas, Highland cattle, Shetland ponies and an African lion born here some years ago. Several picnic sites, wide space for playing games, and a merry-go-round. A miniature railway runs beside a wooded nature trail.

Open 10 a.m.-6 p.m. daily in summer, 11 a.m.-dusk in winter; closed for Christmas holidays. Fee. Refreshments (snack bar and licensed restaurant). WC.

17 BROXBOURNE WOOD, near Broxbourne

Take northbound A10. North of Cheshunt turn on northbound A1170 to Broxbourne, and there turn left at roundabout on westbound minor road signposted Broxbourne Woods. Continue past Baas Hill Common (see earlier entry) along White Stubbs Lane. Between the east and west parking spaces for Bencroft Wood is a minor road to the right, signposted Brickendon Green. This comes out almost opposite the entrance to Broxbourne Wood car-park. There is another car-park on the right along westbound Pembridge lane, with an adjoining picnic site; and one further away in woods beside Cock Lane to the east.

Broxbourne Wood covers some eighty acres of what was once a large local estate. Its traditional stock of oak and hornbeam was replanted in 1960 with conifers, a considerable proportion of which suffered in a fire which broke out during the dry spring of 1974. Today it combines the practical commercial production of timber with recreational amenities. There are four waymarked walks, some conveniently placed seats at intervals, three bridleways and informal picnic sites in addition to the one laid out by the car-park. One path has been devised specially to show the variety of plant life and habitats within the wood. It starts between a stretch of open natural vegetation and a conifer plantation. A few old coppiced hornbeams can still be identified among oak, birch and beech. A number of streams wind their way through the area, crossed by little wooden bridges and flanked by alders, sallows and ferns.

Birds which have been recorded here include blue tits, robins, red polls and willow warblers. Occasionally a muntjac deer may be glimpsed flitting between the trees.

Part of the wood is incorporated in Hertfordshire County Council's imaginative bridleways project for riders and walkers (see following entry).

18 BROXBOURNE WOODS BRIDLEWAYS AND TRAILS

In the Hoddesdon and Broxbourne region the County Council has
collaborated with local councils, with the Countryside Commission
and with a number of volunteers to improve the deteriorating
bridleways and open new circuits for riders and walkers through the
numerous woods and beside the farmlands of south-east
Hertfordshire. These routes embrace a mixture of paths, byways
and public thoroughfares, some of them quiet country roads but
with a few stretches of main highway. Five specified trails have been
waymarked, with yellow markers to indicate when a path is for
pedestrians only. Several of them link up with paths and woodland
described in preceding entries.

Car-parks at Broxbourne Wood, Essendon, Brickendon and
beside the roads at other points offer access to different segments.
One near Goose Green stands at a wooded corner right on the line
of Ermine Street, the Roman highway from London via Royston to
Lincoln. South of the minor road which crosses it is Hoddesdon
Park Wood (see following entry).

19 HODDESDON PARK WOOD, near Hoddesdon

This is part of the same estate which for four hundred years
encompassed Broxbourne, Bencroft and Wormley Woods (see
preceding entries) and, like Wormley, is now classified as a Site of
Special Scientific Interest. It can be reached by minor roads from
those woods already explored; but the most direct route is by the
westbound minor road from Hoddesdon through High Leigh and
Goose Green towards Hertford.

The site, administered by the Woodland Trust, consists in the
main of mature oak woodland, interwoven with paths and rides for
the benefit of the public. The track of Ermine Street divides this
sector from Highfield Wood to the west by a border of pollarded
hornbeams.

20 GREAT WOOD COUNTRYSIDE PARK, Northaw

Take northbound A10. At first roundabout turn left on B198
north-west, then left on westbound B156 towards Cuffley. At
T-junction beyond Cuffley railway station turn right on B157 along

the Ridgeway through beautiful avenues of trees with steep, inviting dells on both sides of the road.

A roadside sign indicates the entrance to the car-park of Great Wood Countryside Park, referred to in some publications and on some maps as Northaw Great Wood, though footpaths through the woods and beside the lake to Northaw itself are in fact south of the Ridgeway.

Seats are nicely set among the bushes around the car-park, all within a most agreeable glade embowered in holly, oak, ferns and soaring silver birch. Three waymarked trails of one, two and three miles lead off into the 540 acres of woodland with large clearings, streams, and ponds.

Nominal parking fee in 'Honour Box'. WC.

Alternative approach: from M25 junction 24 take A111 north-west through Potters Bar and turn right on northbound A1000 to Brookmans Park. There turn right on eastbound B157, the Ridgeway, to Great Wood car-park on the left of the road.

21 COLE GREEN WAY, near Hertford

Take northbound A10 to Hertford, then westbound A414 to Hertingfordbury roundabout. Turn left on southbound minor road to car-park beside old railway track.

This has much in common with the Ayot Greenway (see earlier entry). It consists of a wide track along the abandoned railway route which was once part of the Hertford, Luton and Dunstable line but later served as a branch line between Hertford and Welwyn Garden City. Passenger traffic came to an end in 1951, but freight trains continued to run until 1962. Today one can walk, ride a horse or cycle from Hertford railway viaduct to the A414 between Hatfield and Cole Green. A number of footpaths and bridleways intersect the route at intervals, and minor roads cross it by bridge or tunnel. Near the bridge south of Cole Green is a parking and picnic site.

Most of the accompaniment to the main walk between the banks of the cutting is scrubland, with any number of wild herbs taking over after decades of trimming and – thanks to the steam trains – burning. Nature, always of interest in such surroundings free from intensive cropping and farming, is taking over again and offering different aspects during each season of the year. Insects and butterflies are happily at home among the blackberries, fungi and colourful weeds and flowers; and there is a variety of moss and lichen on the ballast of the track bed.

FROM JUNCTION

26

22 WALTHAM ABBEY

Take westbound A121 signposted into Waltham Abbey.

The environs of the town are now included in the Lee Valley Regional Park (see earlier entry), but the whole place retains enough individuality to deserve separate consideration.

Here is one of England's great historic sites. The abbey itself was founded by King Canute's standard-bearer in the eleventh century and later extended and reconsecrated under the auspices of Harold, briefly King before his defeat by William the Conqueror. His body was brought here for burial behind the high altar, and a statue of him stands at the west front. Alfred, Lord Tennyson lived for a time in Epping Forest, within hearing of the abbey bells, and is believed to have been inspired by them to write the 'Ring out, wild bells' stanzas of *In Memoriam*.

In the grounds are ten acres of enclosed gardens with a moat and fruit trees, and a rose garden on the site of an old farmyard displays over two hundred varieties of roses – pleasant surroundings in which to stroll or picnic. Open meadows stretch away to the north, between B194 and the waters of the Lee and the Cornmill Stream, along what is known locally as the 'Crooked Mile'.

A little way north along this 'Crooked Mile', beside Stubbins Hall Lane is Hayes Hill Farm, opened to the public in 1977. In a setting of largely Victorian farm buildings, different animals are on view in sties, sheds and paddocks. Adults and children are welcome to stroll around and watch farmyard procedures, sheep-shearing, animal-feeding and, on Sundays and Bank Holidays, craft demonstrations in the sixteenth-century timbered barn. Immediately beside Hayes Hill is Holyfieldhall Farm, a working dairy and arable farm of over four hundred acres, with a modern milking parlour in which a herd for Friesian cows are milked every afternoon.

Alternative approach: from M25 junction 25 take southbound A10. At first roundabout, a quarter of a mile to the south, turn left on eastbound A105; at roundabout junction with A1010 turn north and follow signs through Waltham Cross to Waltham Abbey.

Although, as noted at the beginning of this entry, the town's leisure facilities are now regarded as part and parcel of Lee Valley Regional Park, they might with almost equal justice be seen as a fringe benefit of Epping Forest, since the eastbound A121 plunges right into the heart of that forest.

23 EPPING FOREST

Covering such a wide area, this can be approached from several directions from London or Essex according to the driver's personal taste or his own particular point of departure; but so far as the M25 is concerned, there is really only one satisfactory exit, close to the north-west tracts of the forest, after which there are several attractive routes.

From M25 junction 26 take eastbound A121 towards Theydon Bois. At the point of entering the forest, on the junction with a minor road, there is the first of several car-parks. Continue along A121 to the roundabout with A104 and B1393 (the old A11, though road planners wishing to switch traffic to the M11 motorway are determined to erase this original classification from travellers' memories), from which one can explore in all directions.

These six thousand acres were once part of a royal hunting forest which covered all southern Essex between Romford and Great Dunmow, with special privileges for the religious houses at Barking and Waltham. By the eighteenth century much of it had deteriorated into virtual wasteland, used by inhabitants of encroaching villages for common rights, or had been enclosed for farming. Some of the old wildlife remained, however: farmers complained about damage done to their crops by uncontrolled deer who continued to breed in the depths of the woods. There were even wilder and more dangerous forms of life: it was becoming the haunt of fugitives from London justice, hiding themselves and their

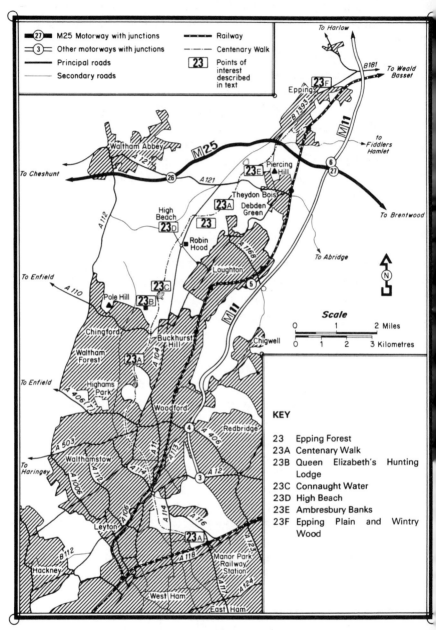

Epping Forest

loot and preying both on the deer and on passers-by.

During the nineteenth century there were many conflicts of interest between commoners mindful of their rights, householders worried by lawlessness, commercial elements eager to exploit the land for building, and conservationists awakening to the need to stem the destruction of the whole character of the forest. Sectors continued to be enclosed in spite of commoners' protests. When a local clergyman decided to fence off a large area to prevent villagers gathering firewood, one Thomas Willingale of Loughton defiantly marched in with his sons and began to lop wood. He was jailed by local magistrates, all of them on the clergyman's side and all of them probably doing a bit of land reclamation on their own. There was such an outcry that the Commons Preservation Society and other bodies took up the case, and the rights and wrongs of it were fought through the courts for fifteen years.

In 1878 the Epping Forest Act appointed the City of London as legal Conservators of the area. It was formally opened to the public on 6 May 1882, when Queen Victoria arrived at Chingford railway station and was driven in an open carriage to High Beach where, after a loyal welcoming address, she declared: 'It gives me the greatest satisfaction to dedicate this beautiful forest to the enjoyment of my people forever.'

Her people had in fact been deriving considerable enjoyment from parts of it long before they were granted official approval. Every Sunday the trippers came flocking in from the East End, a large proportion of them concentrating on the open space of Chingford Plain. A number of fairs were instituted to satisfy their tastes, though they made little appeal to the tastes of local residents. Hooliganism, gang warfare and drunken rioting were just as common then as nowadays. In an effort to encourage a higher moral tone, various organizations began to arrange large-scale Sunday School outings, and teetotallers set up tea gardens and tea tents to compete with the flourishing local pubs. In due course clubs for cricket, golf and football were established.

In our own time so much damage has been done by horse-riding that certain restrictions have been imposed by the Conservators; and there are still some local conflicts over grazing rights and the danger of cattle straying onto the roads. The rasp of cattle-grids under the tyres as one drives into the forest area is a useful reminder of possible hazards ahead, including those from wayward deer. For the casual visitor willing to take to his own two feet, however, there is still a great deal to be enjoyed; scores of open spaces make it easy to park, picnic and saunter away an effortless day; and, descendants of the old tea tents, there are several refreshment kiosks at strategic points along the woodland trails.

23A Centenary Walk

In 1978, to celebrate the hundredth anniversary of the passing of the Epping Forest Act, a fifteen-mile walk was laid out to link the most interesting and attractive parts of the forest. Walkers not wanting to complete the full length of the route can pick it up at any one of a number of chosen points, all of them accessible from main roads and by-roads and from designated parking spaces.

The walk from Manor Park to Epping begins close to the City of London Cemetery – for once a starting point and not a final destination! There is an agreeable amount of open space in the middle of tightly packed streets. A car-park can be found near the Alexandra Lake, beside A146 north of Manor Park railway station. There is another one on Wanstead Flats, beside A114 north of Wanstead park railway station. As well as the line of the Centenary Walk there are plenty of footpaths serving the Flats, Bush Wood and Wanstead Park, with its lavish complement of ponds.

Early stages of the walk, south of Chingford, are hemmed in on a rather narrow belt of greenery, but have some pleasant patches. There are Leyton Flats, with their huge Hollow Pond (parking beside A114 about half a mile north of Green Man roundabout), Walthamstow Forest and Highams Park with its long boating lake. North of A110 the terrain opens out more generously, though at no point more than two miles wide.

Alternative approaches to Centenary Walk: (a) for extreme southern end, from M25 junction 27 take southbound M11 towards London (East), ending at Redbridge roundabout, turn right on westbound A12, and beyond crossroads at Wanstead Underground station turn left on southbound A114 towards Wanstead Park; (b) for Walthamstow Forest, Highams Park and northbound route into the wider stretches of the forest, from M25 junction 27 take southbound M11 towards London (West), joining

A406 but veering left on to Waterworks Corner roundabout, and then take northbound A104 towards Epping, with signposted branches to various locations west of the main road.

Note that although on the map there may at first glance seem to be easy access to the eastern side of Epping Forest from M27 and then M11 junction 5, there is in fact no exit from the southbound M11 at this junction.

23 B   Queen Elizabeth's Hunting Lodge

Now serving as the Epping Forest Museum, this is as good a place as any from which to start a thorough exploration of the area. It stands beside the Rangers Road (A1069) slightly under a mile north-east of Chingford railway station but set in delightful woodland, disdainful of modern urban life. From most directions it is well signposted with the emblem of the Tudor rose. There is a large parking area on the opposite side of the A1069, with a spread of open space behind, and plenty of scope for picnics on the grass or in the shade.

The Centenary Walk includes the museum in its route; but another approach is from the Lee Valley Regional Park (see earlier entry) via M25 junction 25, southbound A10 and eastbound A110 joining eastbound A1069.

The building is recorded as having been completed in 1543 at the command of King Henry VIII, on a site then called Great Standing. The very name makes it clear that this was a vantage point from which to view the pursuit and killing of game, which in fact were driven into an enclosure below the knoll so that the monarch could be assured of a satisfactory spectacle. Construction of the lodge, with its open outer galleries, made it possible to join in with a minimum of exertion by firing down on the doomed beasts. Queen Elizabeth I most probably used it for this purpose; and there is a tradition that on hearing of the defeat of the Spanish Armada she celebrated by riding her white palfrey up the staircase.

In later times it served as the local bailiff's home, and for a while in the nineteenth century as one of the tea houses supplying Sunday trippers, and a shelter for parties of Sunday School children.

When Queen Victoria was due to arrive for the official opening ceremony in 1882, major restoration was put in hand, and a chimneypiece inserted to commemorate the occasion. Since the

Second World War there has been what can only be described as painstaking re-restoration to display as far as possible the building's original features, including its fine roof timbers, and at the same time to house collections of natural history material, forest antiquities, books and records of the region.

To the west, beyond Chingford golf course, an optional diversion of the Centenary Walk takes in Pole Hill. From the Greenwich meridian obelisk on its summit there are views across London and over the reservoirs in the valley below.

Museum open 2 p.m.-6 p.m. (or dusk) Wednesday to Sunday, and Bank Holiday Mondays. Small fee (accompanied children free). Shop. Refreshments at hut or large neighbouring hotel. WC beside hotel.

23C Connaught Water

A short distance east of Queen Elizabeth's Hunting Lodge there is a large car-parking area to the left of the A1069, with walks and picnic spaces around the fine wide expanse of lake, named after the Duke of Connaught, the first forest Ranger – an appointment bestowed on him by his mother, Queen Victoria.

North of the junction of A1069 and A104 there is a parking space to the right of A104; and another one by the Strawberry Hill intersection of the Green Ride footpath and bridleway with a minor road south-east towards Loughton from the Robin Hood roundabout. Interweaving tracks feed into not only the Centenary Walk but also the Three Forests Way, a sixty-mile long-distance path linking the Essex forests of Hatfield, Hainault and Epping.

23D High Beach

This is signposted from the Robin Hood roundabout on A104 and from several other minor junctions in the vicinity. Here the Centenary Walk and the Three Forests Way meet. Epping Forest Conservation Centre is specifically signposted as one draws nearer.

Dick Turpin, a scourge of this as of so many other forest areas, is believed at one time to have used a cave near High Beach as a hideaway. Tennyson lived close by for a period, and it was from here that he heard and was inspired by the bells of Waltham Abbey (see earlier entry). Another poet, Edward Thomas, who loved the Essex countryside, was posted to an army camp here during the

First World War, and found his wife and children a cottage between King's Oak and the Robin Hood. On his last leave before going to his death on the Western Front he was home for Christmas, and his wife sat up half the night 'arranging the greenery that the children had ransacked the forest for during the day'.

In 1970 the Corporation of London decided to contribute to European Conservation Year by establishing a Field Studies Centre at High Beach. There had already been facilities for naturalists and other specialized groups, but the intention now was to encourage the general public, especially children, to add to their own enjoyment by studying the forest and its environmental problems. Under the auspices of the Field Studies Council, the Conservation Centre copes with the need of school groups, teachers and individuals with specific interests, and with enquiries from visitors of all kinds and ages.

Facing the centre is a huge car-park, surrounded by picnic areas and radiating a number of walks into the woods. The centre itself mounts varying exhibitions and has a public information desk with maps, guides, and other items of local interest for sale, open every day except Monday and Tuesday. Close at hand are a refreshment kiosk and the Duke of Wellington pub. WC.

23E Ambresbury Banks

Where the northbound B1393 towards Epping is joined from the left by a minor road from Upshire, woods opposite the junction conceal the surviving earthworks of an Iron Age fort covering some twelve acres. A rampart about six feet high is surrounded by a ditch almost ten feet deep and twenty feet across. It is so much overgrown by vegetation that one can easily miss the significance of its contours.

This is not the only ancient fortification within the forest. Towards the eastern fringe is the rather less substantial fort of Loughton Camp, not particularly impressive in itself but near some very attractive viewpoints.

23F Epping Plain and Wintry Wood

This is pretty well the last wooded enclave, north of the town of Epping itself, before the Essex farmlands take over. Footpaths and bridleways cut across a triangle encompassed by the B1393, the eastbound B181 through North Weald toward Chelmsford, and a minor road joining these two. There is a parking space beside a minor road turning right from B1393 towards Coopersale.

Near Epping Underground station begins the sixty-five-mile Essex Way to Dedham on the borders of Suffolk.

Alternative approach to Epping Plain and Wintry Wood, and to Epping Forest in north-south direction: from M25 junction 27 take northbound M11, and at M11 junction 7 take southbound B139 through Thornwood Common to Epping.

JUNCTIONS
26-30

Although it is possible by using the northbound M11 to reach a fair distance into Cambridgeshire in well under the hour, to walk on the Gog Magog Hills and even explore the fringes of Suffolk, there is otherwise little free-ranging open space for the casual visitor within sensible driving range in that direction. Sites in this chapter are therefore predominantly in Essex and the eastern outskirts of Greater London.

Access to a large number of them is from the A12, a trunk road which for many years was notorious for its cramped single-lane traffic, poor surface and frequent bottlenecks. In recent years most of these snags have been ironed out, and the worst stretch of all around Chelmsford is being superseded by a bypass due for completion towards the end of 1986. This means that there will be dual carriageway the whole distance from Brentwood M25/A12 interchange to Ipswich, and along a large part of the westbound A12 into London. Drivers made suspicious by memories of past delays should take heart and give this road a second chance.

Essex is not quite such a flat county as some of its critics claim. There are long vistas of gently undulating countryside whose mixtures of farmland and low, tree-spattered ridges are very restful to the eye; and the vast overpowering sky can offer cloudscapes as dramatic as those of remoter East Anglia and the coast. Traffic on the minor roads is usually sparser than in the other regions we have dealt with, and few of the woodlands and other spaces recommended here are far from some bright, hospitable little town or village: Harlow, Southend and Clacton are far from representing all that Essex has to offer the day visitor or holidaymaker.

KEY

1   Hainault Forest Park
2   Havering-atte-Bower Country Park
3   Hatfield Forest
4   Mole Hill Wildlife Park, near Newport
5   Weald Country Park, near Brentwood
6   Thorndon Country Park (North), near Ingrave
7   Thorndon Country Park (South), near Herongate
'8   Hylands Park, Writtle
9   Danbury Country Park
10   Danbury and Lingwood Commons
11   Abberton Reservoir, near Mersea
12   Cudmore Grove Country Park, East Mersea
13   Dunton Plotland Trail, near Basildon
14   Langdon Hills Country Park, near Basildon
15   Norsey Wood, Billericay
16   Hanningfield Reservoir, near Billericay
17   Marsh Farm Country Park, South Woodham Ferrers
18   Belhus Woods Country Park, Aveley
19   Coalhouse Fort, East Tilbury

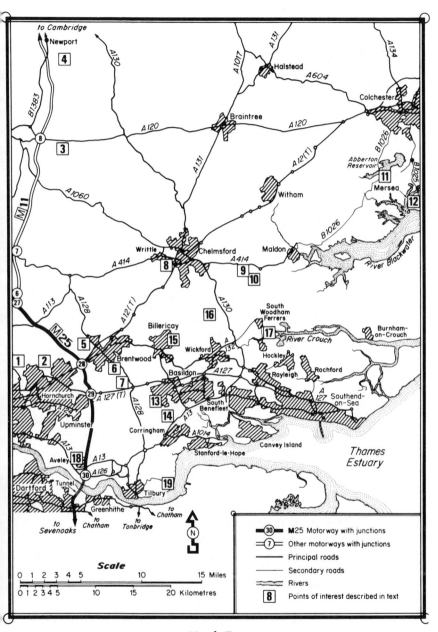

North-East

1 HAINAULT FOREST PARK

Take eastbound A121 and A1168 south-east towards Chigwell. Under M11 flyover turn left on A113 towards Ongar, then right on A1112 signposted Chigwell Row and cross traffic lights by the Maypole inn. The main entrance to the forest park is on the left just before a pedestrian bridge across the road. There are a number of parking spaces within the grounds.

An alternative approach is to turn left at the traffic lights by the Maypole along Lambourne Road, and use smaller car-park a short distance along on the right.

The 'forest' is in fact largely open space with smoothly sloping expanses of grass, broken by patches of gorse and of deciduous woodland made up of oak, beech, birch, hawthorn and arthritic, contorted hornbeams. In 1774 Hainault Forest amounted to almost five thousand acres, but it was gradually nibbled away by enclosure until in 1851 most of the remaining trees were grubbed up, leaving only a few ancient oaks and hornbeams. Attempts were made in Parliament seven years later to encourage reafforestation, but by then only a few hundred acres remained. Fortunately Edward North Buxton, whose enlightened work with the Commons Preservation Society had done so much to safeguard Epping Forest (see Chapter 7), set about organizing funds for purchasing and replenishing some eight hundred acres of the forest, and in 1903 the Hainault Act designated it an open space, expanded to a thousand acres, for recreational purpose in perpetuity.

Today it boasts two full-size eighteen-hole golf courses, open to the public seven days a week, with green fees set at a reasonable level and clubs for hire from the course professional. There are also football and cricket pitches, a horse ride of over four miles, and a six-acre fishing lake. The Thames Water Authority issues fishing licences for catching carp, tench, perch, roach and pike with rod and reel. Anglers do not seem to disturb the plentiful birdlife on the water and its little island.

Nobody needs, however, to be too strenuous. The forest park is extensive enough to allow for uninterrupted leisurely walking, and at intervals there are groups of picnic tables and benches. Children will enjoy the animal paddocks with goats, Shetland ponies, donkeys, llamas, ducks, geese and chickens.

The Yard Office beside the main car-park provides information leaflets concerning the forest and other local amenities.

Refreshment kiosk and golf club restaurant. WC.

The Three Forests Way linking Hatfield, Hainault and Epping (see Epping Forest entry in Chapter 7) runs through the park and *en route* provides a link with Havering-atte-Bower Country Park a mile and a half to the east (see following entry).

Alternative approach to Hainault Forest: from M2 junction 28 take westbound A12 through Romford towards London. Turn right on northbound A1112 towards Chigwell. The main entrance is on the right beyond the pedestrian bridge over the road. This same route can be picked up from M25 junction 29 along westbound A127 to join A12 at Gallows Corner, then continuing as above.

2 HAVERING-ATTE-BOWER COUNTRY PARK

Take eastbound A121 and B172 through Theydon Bois to Abridge. Turn left on northbound A113 towards Ongar, and then right on southbound B175 to Havering-atte-Bower.

The road runs between several large areas of open space, including Pyrgo Park (with Bedford's Park and Broxhill Common to the south) on one side, and the country park on the right. This 165-acre park is a fairly informal one, with a number of plantations, plenty of grassy picnic space, bridleways and a nature trail. WC.

There is a footpath link of a mile and a half with Hainault Forest Country Park (see preceding entry).

Alternative approach: from M25 junction 28 take westbound A12, and in Romford turn right on northbound B175 to country park. The same route can be picked up from M25 junction 29 along westbound A127 to join A12 at Gallows Corner and B175 in Romford.

3 HATFIELD FOREST

Take northbound M11 towards Cambridge. At M11 junction 8 take eastbound A120 towards Braintree. In Takeley Street a minor road to the right is signposted Hatfield Forest, and the entrance to the forest car-park is signposted to the right a short distance along this. There is a fee for cars (free to National Trust members), but this allows one to make a long, winding drive through woodlands to the banks of a wide, tree-girt lake with benches and picnic tables on its grassy banks, and a roofed-in picnic area for rainy or gusty days.

This was part of the great royal hunting forest of Essex even before the Norman Conquest. Among the massive oaks and hornbeams is a millstone with a plaque marking the site of the Old Doodle Oak, supposedly eight hundred years of age when it finally came down in 1924 and quite possibly the very oak shown in the Domesday Book survey. Early in the thirteenth century local inhabitants carried out disafforestation of the northern edge, and from then on there was more and more encroachment on royal hunting rights. Unlike other parts of the dismembered forest such as Epping and Hainault, however, Hatfield retained many of its chases, hunting rides and ancient coppices. For two centuries they were in the hands of one family, the Houblons, until the break-up of their estates just after the First World War.

That same Edward North Buxton who had salvaged much of the threatened remains of Epping and Hainault forests (see earlier entries) heard in 1923 that Hatfield's woodlands were to be completely levelled by a timber merchant, and again came to the rescue – with the last cheque he ever wrote. After his death Hatfield Forest was handed over into the keeping of the National Trust, with later gifts bringing the total area up to more than a thousand acres.

In spring the glades are aglow with primroses, oxlip and anemones. They and their surroundings form a paradise for bird-watchers, so rich and varied that for ten years the Bishop's Stortford Natural History Society Bird Group kept up regular observation and prepared a census of breeding patterns, numbers and location of the forest birds. The lake and its banks form a sort of community centre for ducks, moorhens, teal, mallard, water rail, reed bunting and even the nightingale.

Shell House by the lake was built in 1759 by the Houblons as a summerhouse, inset with flints, shells and glass chippings. Today it contains a small exhibition of coppicing and general forest maintenance, and a small National Trust shop open at weekends. Tickets are issued here for boating, and for fishing in the lake and a smaller decoy lake, offering between them a selection of roach, rudd, perch, tench, carp and large pike.

North of the lake is a nature reserve. A nature trail of about a mile and a half starts from Shell House and takes in some interesting plant life around the fenced-off marshy area managed by the Essex Naturalists' Trust.

In the woods of Beggarshall Coppice stand the Portingbury Hills, in reality a hummock of little more than five feet high, but a hundred feet across, an earthwork most probably dating from the Iron Age.

Hatfield stands at one end of the Three Forests Way threading through Havering and Hainault and into Epping (see earlier entries for Epping and Hainault Forests, and for Havering-atte-Bower).

Refreshments beside the lake, open most days. WC.

4 MOLE HILL WILDLIFE PARK, near Newport

Take northbound M11 towards Cambridge. At M11 junction 8 take north-west turn-off and pick up northbound B1383 through Stansted Mountfichet towards Newport. Turn right on eastbound minor road signposted to Widdington, and follow signs to the Wildlife Reserve.

In the grounds of a moated Elizabethan hall near Debden and Widdington (the house itself not open to the public), first recorded in the thirteenth century as Molehalle, a collection of mammals and birds in pools and enclosures was started in 1948 and opened in 1964.

There is a picnic site in the grounds.

Open 10.30 a.m.-6 p.m. or dusk daily, except Christmas Day. Fee (children half-price, children under 2 free). Shop. Refreshments. WC.

NEARBY FEATURES:

Audley End (AM). Reached by continuing north on B1383 to signposted entrance on the right. 'Too large for a King, but might do well for a Lord Treasurer,' James I is reported as saying dourly when first invited to see the building by his Lord High Treasurer, later committed to the Tower of London on charges of embezzlement. Much of it was later pulled down or modified, but the Jacobean stable block survives; there are sumptuous furnishings in the state rooms, and a miniature railway runs through part of the extensive grounds. Open 1 p.m.-6 p.m. daily except Monday (but open Bank Holiday Mondays) April to September. Grounds open noon. Fee. Refreshments. WC.

Linton Zoological Gardens. Continue north to roundabout junction with A11, follow A11 north-east, and at next roundabout turn right signposted Linton Zoo; or from B1383 north of Mole Hill Wildlife Park turn right on B1052 to Linton crossroads and follow sign to Linton Zoo.

FROM JUNCTION

28

5 WEALD COUNTRY PARK, near Brentwood

Take eastbound A1023 towards Brentwood and turn left on minor road northbound over A12 to South Weald. At T-junction there are car-parks in either direction: one beside the cricket ground to the right of the junction, others to the left by the Wardens' houses beside Weald Road towards Coxtie Green, and one some distance from that same road on the edge of a lake and marshy area.

South Weald estate was once an endowment of Harold's to Waltham Abbey, and remained in the care of that foundation even after the many readjustments made by William the Conqueror. Part of the property included the insignificant little hamlet of Brentwood, now of much greater size. Since the land was not especially fertile it was used in the main as a deer park, and large tracts of this remained complete with their herds of deer until just before the Second World War. After the Dissolution of the Monasteries, the Treasurer of King Henry VIII's Household took possession and built himself a mansion here. All that remains of this is a cottage in what used to be its garden, where Mary Tudor is reputed have kept what we now call a 'low profile' during a period of anti-Catholic feeling: the building is still known as Queen Mary's Chapel.

In the eighteenth century work began on an ambitious scheme for landscaping the park, and although this was left incomplete there are still echoes of its design around the Belvedere mound, on which stood a folly 'temple' to which later owners added an incongruous castellated upper storey. During the Second World War the park was used for Home Guard training, with a mortar range. In the run-up to D-Day it became an assembly point for troops, as a result of which the enclosed deer park ceased to exist: fences were taken apart to allow vehicles through, and all the animals fled into the surrounding countryside. Wild fallow deer, their descendants, are still to be found around Brentwood and Ongar, and some have found their way back into Weald Park.

Soon after the war the dilapidated hall and the Belvedere were demolished. All that remains of the hall is a flight of garden steps; of the Belvedere, its mound like a squat Norman motte.

Even the very ground was at one time despoiled. A sudden rush of ploughing late in 1948 devastated over a hundred acres of ancient grassland, but fortunately the mightiest of the old trees were spared.

The lakes were formed in the middle of the eighteenth century by damming a brook. They are now a popular venue for fishermen, and for moorhens who breed here. A resident flock of Canada geese summer on a small lake across Weald Road and winter on the larger one.

Late in the nineteenth century, when the area known as 'The Forest' was fenced off as a protection against roaming deer, a fine avenue of horse chestnut was laid down. It is now in its prime. Strolling along it is a great joy at any time of the year, and there are other plantations and inviting glades to either side. Planting is carefully managed nowadays to provide a variety of species for the pleasure of the visitor.

A hill fort known as South Weald Camp hunches up above Sandpits Lane on the western edge of the park. It was a single earthen bank and ditch around a level patch of about seven acres. No archaeological research has been carried out on it, but it is thought to date from some time after 500 BC.

What may at the moment look none too picturesque is in fact scheduled as a future amenity: Coxtie landfill site beside the park is at present a County Council refuse tip but, as the dumping continues, the hills so formed are covered with soil ready for seeding and for planting trees. Much of its stock is likely to come from the Weald Park Tree Nursery, where some twenty thousand young trees are nurtured ready for use all over Essex.

Picnic areas have been sited within reasonable distance of the car-parks, easy of access by push-chairs and even wheelchairs. Guided walks of about an hour and a half start 10.30 a.m. every Sunday from the Visitor Centre.

Open daily 7 a.m. until half an hour after sunset. Small parking fee charged at weekends from April to October. Day fishing permits obtainable from the water bailiff at the upper lake; season tickets, and permits for horse riding, obtainable from the Parks Office beside the second entrance off northbound Weald Road. WC by cricket ground and Belvedere car-parks, and in copse east of the Tree Nursery entrance.

6 THORNDON COUNTRY PARK (NORTH), near Ingrave

Take eastbound A1023 into Brentwood. At traffic lights in centre of town turn right on southbound A128. Entrance to the country park is signposted along minor road to the right in Ingrave.

The approach to the actual entrance is most impressive. Successive members of the Petre family from the sixteenth century onwards built mansions here, demolished and rebuilt, landscaped the grounds and gave assistance to Roman Catholic families and churches in the region, until the sixteenth Lord Petre died in the First World War, after which the estate was split up. The eighteenth-century Thorndon Hall now stands derelict close to the main road through Ingrave, but its western approach carriage drive is still graced by the Lion Lodge and its tall gateposts each bearing a stone lion, guarding the way into the country park.

Large tracts of the old parkland have survived, with ancient hornbeams and oaks. One remarkable specimen is an unpollarded tree known as the 'crinoline lady' because of its 'skirt' of scar tissue around the lower trunk, where deer came to rub the velvet off their antlers. Childerditch Wood was common land until the late eighteenth century, when it was planted with oaks. Later, conifers were added, but there was wholesale felling in our own century, and it is only since the establishment of the country park that modern management, including regular coppicing and proper care for the habitats of the varying wildlife, has brought it under control. It is now being built up as high oak woodland, sheltering shrubs such as hazel, hawthorn and holly, and an appreciative community of birds.

Childerditch Pond, one of three artificial pools in the two Thorndon Country Parks, North and South, was cleared out by German prisoners of war during the First World War. By 1976 it had been so neglected that plants and weeds had choked it, and there was no water left. Since then it has been cleaned out again and the water level restored, now maintained for its plant and wildlife interest.

The names of Childerditch and of Cockridden Farm to the south recall the wistful promise in the poem by Edward Thomas, a great lover of this countryside, that 'when sufficiently rich' he would give 'Codham, Cockridden and Childerditch, Roses, Pyrgo and Lapwater' to his elder daughter. Guided walks of about an hour and a half start at 2.30 p.m. every Sunday from the first car-park.

Open daily 7 a.m. until half an hour after sunset. Small car-parking fee at weekends from April to October. Information hut at main car-park. WC at main car-park.

A public footpath to Thorndon Country Park (South) begins on the eastern edge of the park.

Alternative approach: from M25 junction 29 take eastbound A127 towards Southend. At interchange by the Halfway House inn turn left on northbound A128, past entrance to Thorndon Country Park (South), and continue to Ingrave and signposted minor road to the left.

7 THORNDON COUNTRY PARK (SOUTH), near Herongate
From M25 junction 28 follow directions as for preceding entry, but continue on southbound A128 through Ingrave and Herongate. Entrance to the southern park is signposted to the right of the road, just before interchange with A127.

This was originally an integral part of the same estate as the northern park, and its woodlands have much in common, though the fine open spaces of grassland are due to recent reclamation from agricultural use. Overlooking the grass is the Octagon Plantation, a survivor of the early-eighteenth-century landscaping in which, inevitably, 'Capability' Brown took a hand.

Ruins of the original Tudor hall are to be found in Ruins Wood. Close at hand is Old Hall Pond, dammed in the sixteenth century to serve a watermill which once stood here, but later cleaned out and integrated into the over-all landscaping. Today it is maintained as open water for fishing, with some little colonies of floating and rooted plants.

Open daily 7 a.m. until half an hour after sunset. Small car-parking fee at weekends from April to October. Day fishing permits obtainable from the warden at Old Hall Pond. Vehicles with disabled anglers are allowed access to the pond by arrangements with the warden. WC (by Octagon Plantation).

A public footpath to Thorndon Country Park (North) begins at the north-western edge of the park.

Alternative approach: from M25 junction 29 take eastbound A127 towards Southend. At interchange by the Halfway House inn turn left on northbound A128. Entry to the car-park is signposted a short distance up on the left.

8 HYLANDS PARK, Writtle
Take eastbound A12 towards Chelmsford. The long brick wall of Hylands Park flanks this road as it climbs to the dominating landmark spire of Widford church. One can follow the dual carriageway this far to the first of Chelmsford's many roundabouts, and turn left to follow signposts to Writtle; but it makes a pleasanter drive to leave the A12 by a minor road to the left signposted Writtle.

There is no entrance to the huge park from the A12. One needs to wend a way through the delightful village of Writtle, with its broad green and pond – not, as it may seem, a duck or horse pond but one created for the needs of traction engines on the local roads – into Paradise Road. The sumptuous park is open daily, so free and easy that it comes as quite a shock to find an eighteenth-century mansion resplendent in its grounds, sadly unoccupied since 1962. There are walks through acres of woodland, and some gleaming lakes to set off the green spaces of what was once among the many manors held by Harold of Wessex, powerful over the East Saxons as over the West.

9 DANBURY COUNTRY PARK

Take eastbound A12 to Chelmsford and then eastbound A414 towards Maldon. On the outskirts of Danbury the country park is signposted down a minor road to the right. There are two car-parks on the left of this road: one by Danbury Lakes with a pleasant view across the water, and reasonably easy access to the lakeside walks for wheelchairs; the other a short distance to the east, with a well-marked path to the lakes and a small picnic site. A common sight here is that of bold squirrels sitting on the waste bin foraging for scraps.

The expanses of water were once part of the ornamental gardens of Danbury Place, an early nineteenth-century building once belonging to the bishops of Rochester but now a management training centre. The house is not open to the public but can be seen from the country park which has been developed in its grounds.

There are broad paths around the lakes, with a number of seats at intervals. On the northern slopes behind, paths lead onto a large grassy picnic and play area. The gardens are bright with herbaceous borders, and in season the great banked-up rhododendrons are a blaze of unbroken beauty. Those seeking peace and quiet will find many a sheltered woodland corner, and there is plenty of birdlife to observe: one section of the woods is noted for its nightingales.

Fishing is allowed on two of the lakes by day permit. From mid-May until the end of September there are guided walks of about an hour and a half starting from the Lakes car-park, details of which are displayed on the car-park noticeboards during the season.

Alternative approach: from M25 junction 29 take eastbound

A127; turn left on northbound A130 towards Chelmsford, right on eastbound B1012, and left on northbound B1418 towards Woodham Mortimer, turning off left on minor road to the country park.

10 DANBURY and LINGWOOD COMMONS

Take eastbound A12 to Chelmsford and then eastbound A414 towards Maldon. At Danbury, either turn right on minor road signposted for country park and drive past the park to a junction with minor roads on a corner of the commons, or continue through Danbury itself and at its eastern end turn right on minor road signposted Danbury Common.

There is parking space on the right of this road, and the National Trust provides other spaces on the common land below, beside the road towards Woodham Ferrers.

Both stretches of heather, bracken and brambles, with rather more trees and secluded glades on Lingwood than on Danbury Common, are survivors of the great Essex forest and of days when commoners of the surrounding settlements could put their animals out to graze and collect firewood. It is difficult to think of a greater contrast, within such a small compass, than that between the formal gardens and ornamental lakes of Danbury Place and Country Park (see preceding entry) and these 215 acres of untamed, ancient land. Neolithic flints have been unearthed from Beacon Hill, the highest point, and the region cannot have changed markedly since the tenth century, when it was a royal hunting demesne. It is all well served with footpaths, and tracts for rough open walking. One much-trodden footpath leads north-west through Blakes Wood, with a treasury of wild flowers in a setting of chestnut coppice and hornbeams, and onto the Heather Hills above Little Baddow, with a seat on top from which to contemplate the view.

Danbury had an army camp of some consequence towards the end of the eighteenth century and through the Napoleonic Wars: at one time there were fourteen regiments stationed here. The parapet of a redoubt built during that period can still be found among the gorse and bracken on one rim of the common, beside the Sandon road.

Alternative approach: from M25 junction 29 take eastbound

A127; turn left on northbound A130 towards Chelmsford, right on eastbound B1012, and left on northbound B1418 towards Woodham Mortimer, when parking spaces for the commons will be found on the right of the road below Danbury.

11 ABBERTON RESERVOIR, near Mersea

This and the following entry are on the extreme edge of our agreed itinerary in this direction, but by no means out of reach.

Take eastbound A12 past Chelmsford. At Hatfield Peverel take southbound B1019 to Maldon, and then B1026 north-east towards Colchester, crossing the reservoir.

The wild bird sanctuary here has a hide available to the public by permit, and coarse fishing by permit. For the casual visitor there is ample car-parking space and a picnic site, with walks along the banks of the reservoir.

NEARBY FEATURES:

Layer Marney Tower. This can be reached from a minor westbound road through Layer Breton, between B1026 and B1022. A superb sixteenth-century red brick gatehouse and two wings, including a two-storeyed long gallery, remain from the great house built by King Henry VIII's Keeper of the Privy Seal, set in spacious gardens. Open 2 p.m.-6 p.m. Sunday and Thursday, April to September; also Tuesdays during July and August, and Bank Holiday weekends 11 a.m.-6 p.m. Fee (reduced for children, and under school age free). Shop. WC.

Colchester Zoo. At Stanway Hall, signposted off B1022. Lions, tigers and other animals; a reptile house, aquarium and birdland. Picnic site, miniature railway and amusements in the parkland of a stylish hall rebuilt in the sixteenth century.

Open daily 9.30 a.m.-dusk in summer, 10 a.m.-4 p.m. in winter. Fee. Refreshments. Shop. WC.

12 CUDMORE GROVE COUNTRY PARK, East Mersea

Take eastbound A12 to Chelmsford and A414 to Maldon, then B1026 north-east and follow signs to Mersea. The park is set off Bromans Lane in East Mersea.

This was classified as a country park and opened by Essex County Council in 1975, enclosing large spreads of grassland for picnics and games – kite-flying is an especially rewarding pastime here, utilizing the sea breezes – and a number of plantations including stands of oak along the seaward edge, framing views over the River Colne. A small sandy beach is reached by means of a broad ramp. From here the oyster smacks can be seen dredging the oyster beds, and there is an intermittent passage of cargo vessels to and from Colchester docks. Added to this during the summer is the incomparable sight of Thames barges with their characteristic sails, heading in or out of Brightlingsea. For closer inspection, many splendid specimens of the classic barges are laid up at Maldon, not too far away.

Near to the car-park an old gravel pit has become known as the Dell, allowed to grow wild and offer a welcome to any number of butterflies. In the south-eastern corner of the park is a nature reserve established by the Nature Conservancy Council over an area of low-lying salt marsh and shallow water where Brent geese and other wildfowl come to feed, and varied species of wader plop and peck their way along the shore. Visitors are admitted into the reserve but are particularly asked to keep to the paths provided and not disturb the birds or plant life.

Open daily 8 a.m.-dusk, all year round. WC.

Alternative approach: from M25 junction 29 take eastbound A127 towards Southend; turn north-east on A132 through Wickford, then follow signs through Maldon to Mersea.

FROM JUNCTION

29

13 DUNTON PLOTLAND TRAIL, near Basildon

Take eastbound A127. At Dunton interchange take southbound B148 towards Laindon, then immediately right on southbound minor road towards Horndon on the Hill. Some distance along Lower Dunton Road a car-park for the Plotland Trail is signposted to the left.

Early in this century large tracts of poor agricultural land were bought up by property developers and sold off piecemeal by auction. Between the First and Second World Wars many families bought land and built their holiday and weekend bungalows here. Now only a few of these are left, looking somewhat forlorn in the middle of derelict sites and the ghostly outlines of old properties. The Plotland Trail has been laid out for informal recreation and to show the pattern of a development so very diferent from modern town housing complexes.

One main trail has waymarked posts, but there are other optional routes along grassy avenues between the ruins of former houses and abandoned gardens: in many places, stubborn garden flowers can be seen struggling for survival among the wild plants which have invaded their once tidy world, and rabbits and foxes have not been slow to make their homes in forgotten corners.

14 LANGDON HILLS COUNTRY PARK, near Basildon

Take eastbound A127. At Dunton interchange take B148 south and east into Laindon. Turn right on southbound B1007 towards Langdon Hills.

There are basically two sections to the country park: Westley Heights and, a short distance south-east, One Tree Hill, linked by footpaths and bridleways. Both are well supplied with parking and picnic spaces.

The Langdon Hills were used by many kinds and generations of men before being comfortably drawn into the leisure area of today. Fragments of Bronze Age axes and Iron Age pots have been found in the neighbourhood, especially around One Tree Hill, and in Basildon itself an iron foundry was discovered. Excavated material from the whole area, along with agricultural and local industrial collections, can be seen in the Thurrock Museum, Orsett Road, Grays (admission free, open 10 a.m.-8 p.m. Monday to Friday, 10 a.m.-5 p.m. Saturday, closed Bank Holidays, all year round).

In medieval times the manor of Westley laid out a deer park, and there are still traces of the woodland banks and accompanying ditches constructed to keep deer out of the coppiced woodlands. Early in our own century, brushwood faggots from the coppices were used in the foundations of oil storage tanks on the marshes below.

Building grew apace after the First World War, and the unspoilt heights were so seriously threatened that the County Council bought large tracts to establish a designated Open Space in 1932. During the Second World War there was a refugee camp at the corner of High Road and Dry Street, later converted into a prisoner-of-war camp. This is now a grassy car-park.

All well as the open grassland for leisure activity, there are some remarkable flower meadows within the park: the uniqueness of Martinhole Meadow has led to its being classified as a Site of Special Scientific Interest, containing as it does rarities such as the green-veined orchid and adder's tongue fern – to be admired from a proper distance, as with their colourful companions, but *not* picked or damaged.

Some of the woodland is ancient. Other plantations have been recently established on arable land which was intensively cultivated during the Second World War. Below and around the old and new stands are seasonal displays of bluebells, wood anemones and primroses. The presence of a large number of ponds is due partly to the once flourishing brick and tile works in the locality. This industry, prosperous towards the end of the last century, dwindled away in the early years of this one, leaving as a visible memento only a large sandpit, a few overgrown spoil heaps, and the ponds which were soon choked with weeds and are only now being fully restored. The two main tile kilns were on the site now occupied by the One Tree Hill WC.

Information concerning the country park is displayed on stands at the One Tree Hill and Westley Heights car-parks. Regular patrolling wardens are glad to answer questions. Guided walks of about an hour and a half start at 10.30 a.m. every Sunday from the One Tree Hill information centre, and other walks or events such as cross-country running and orienteering programmes are announced on the information stands.

Open daily until dusk, all year round. Ice cream on sale during summer weekends. WC.

Alternative approach: from M25 junction 30 take eastbound A13 towards Basildon. About two miles beyond interchange at Stanford-le-Hope turn left on minor northbound road to parking for One Tree Hill.

15 NORSEY WOOD, Billericay

Take eastbound A127 towards Southend. On outskirts of Basildon turn left on northbound A176 and A1007 into Billericay. The wood lies beside a minor road north-east from the centre of the town, off B1007.

There are sixty-six acres of ancient coppiced woodland with footpaths, picnic glades, a nature reserve and nature trail. On the southern fringe of the wood is a prehistoric tumulus, and in the neighbourhood there have been many Romano-British finds, most of them swallowed up by the modern town.

Alternative approach: from M25 junction 28 take eastbound A1023 through Brentwood. In Shenfield take eastbound A129 to Billericay, turn left on northbound B1007, and right on minor road to Norsey Wood.

16 HANNINGFIELD RESERVOIR, near Billericay

Take eastbound A127 towards Southend. On outskirts of Basildon turn left on northbound A176 and A1007 into Billericay, and then take minor road north-east past Norsey Wood (see preceding entry) and Ramsden Heath to Hanningfield.

From the Fishing Lodge one can obtain permits for rowing on the lake, and for coarse fishing. There are walks along the banks, and a wild bird sanctuary which also requires a permit. Open daily. WC.

Alternative approach: from M25 junction 28 take eastbound A12. At interchange north-east of Brentwood take B1002 to Ingatestone, then turn right on minor road to Stock and minor road to Hanningfield.

17 MARSH FARM COUNTRY PARK, South Woodham
   Ferrers

Take eastbound A127 towards Southend. Beyond Basildon take northbound A130 towards Chelmsford, then turn right on eastbound B1012 towards South Woodham Ferrers. At succession of roundabouts in the new town area follow signs to the country park.

There is plenty of parking space here, and beside the car-park a large picnic area has been provided with benches and tables.

A small fee is payable for entry to the country park itself, which is built around a working farm set between the new streets of the town and the atmospheric salt marshes by the River Crouch, and incorporates three miles of riverside walks. All the farm buildings have been provided with walkways and viewpoints so that visitors can get a good look at every aspect of traditional and modern livestock farming, with the farm staff themselves all qualified to explain the different procedures. In addition there are information boards and, in the Visitor Centre, displays and audio-visual programmes. As well as the outdoor picnic site there is indoor picnic accommodation.

At the eastern end of the park is a wildlife conservation zone, a haven for wintering birds with a specially expanded lake and wet meadows surrounding it. A public footpath overlooking this reserve runs along the sea wall, and there are plans for constructing more hides for public use.

Open 10 a.m.-4 p.m. Monday to Friday, 10 a.m.-5 p.m. weekends and Bank Holidays all year round. WC.

FROM JUNCTION
30

18 BELHUS WOODS COUNTRY PARK, Aveley

Take eastbound A13 towards Basildon. At first interchange turn north and west through North Stifford, right on northbound B186, and left on westbound B1335 to Aveley. At roundabout in centre of Aveley turn right on northbound minor road towards Upminster. The car-park for Belhus Woods is on the right just over a mile north.

Here are 140 acres of woodland and lakes, with footpaths and bridleways through such agreeably named plantations as Running Water Wood and Little Brick-kiln Wood, the latter recalling a once busy industry here. The atmosphere remains attractively rural in spite of the crowding in of Dagenham, Romford and Purfleet, the

Long-distance footpaths

chimneys of the chalk workings, and the proximity of the pulsing M25 on its way down towards the Dartford Tunnel.

Guided walks of about an hour and a half start at 10.30 a.m. every Sunday from the Visitor Centre. Open daily throughout the year. WC.

Alternative approach: from M25 junction 29 take eastbound A127 towards Southend. At flyover take southbound B186 through South Ockendon and turn right on westbound B1335 to Aveley, then follow directions as above.

Note: there is no direct westbound exit from northbound carriageway on the A13 at junction 30; and on southbound carriageway junctions 30 and 31 exits are combined.

19 COALHOUSE FORT, East Tilbury

Take eastbound A13 towards Basildon. Approaching Stanford-le-Hope, turn right on southbound minor road through East Tilbury to Coalhouse Fort car-park.

The fort itself is a dilapidated Victorian building set up in the 1869 by Royal Engineers from Gravesend under their then commander, General Gordon of later fame at Khartoum. The area around the bleak grey stonework has been converted into a bright, attractive park with flowerbeds, gorse bushes, benches, a children's playground and boats for hire. It is an admirable place for studying, if not the ranks of oil-storage tanks, at any rate the ever-changing pattern of River Thames shipping. WC.

Not far to the west, but attainable only by means of a network of minor roads across the marshes, are the more substantial remains of the earlier Tilbury Fort (AM). The original fort was ordered by King Henry VIII as part of his coastal defence system. It was here that his daughter Elizabeth reviewed her troops as the Spanish Armada approached, and in her speech made one of her most famous declarations: 'I have the body of a weak and feeble woman, but I have the heart and stomach of a king, and of a king of England too.' Later the fortifications were rebuilt and strengthened against possible Dutch attacks, and against the threat of a Napoleonic invasion.

Open 9.30 a.m.-4 p.m. weekdays, 2 p.m.-4 p.m. Sunday, mid-October to mid-March; 9.30 a.m.-6.30 p.m. weekdays, 2 p.m.-6.30 p.m. Sunday, mid-March to mid-October. Small fee.

ACKNOWLEDGEMENTS

At various stages of my explorations I have been helped by a number of individuals generous with their time and advice, though in too many cases I do not even know their names. I am nevertheless grateful to them, and equally grateful to a few old friends who offered not just help but accommodation and hospitality: Gill and Laurence Vulliamy, Maureen and John Tingle, Jenny and Francis Hadfield, and, not for the first time, Shirley and John Tustin.

The following local organizations were all swift and friendly in answering my queries and offering guidance:

Bracknell County Library
Essex County Council Parks Office
Hertfordshire County Council Planning Officer
Kent County Council
Rochester upon Medway Tourist Information Centre
South East England Tourist Board
Thames and Chilterns Tourist Board

There are also those organizations which should be thanked not merely for specific help on this project but for their continuing contributions to the welfare of our countryside in general:

The Commons, Open Spaces and Footpath Preservation Society
The Countryside Commission
The Forestry Commission
The National Trust
The Nature Conservancy Council
The Open Spaces Society
The Woodland Trust

SELECT BIBLIOGRAPHY

Walks and long-distance paths

AA Book of Country Walks (Drive Publications)

Along the Chiltern Ways, G.R. Crosher (Cassell)

Chalkways of South and South-East England, Edward C. Pyatt (David & Charles)

Climbing and Walking in South-East England, Edward C. Pyatt (David & Charles)

Concise Guide to the Footpaths of Britain (Collins)

The Greensand Way (Surrey Amenity Council, Guildford)

Guide to the London Countryway, Keith Chesterton (Constable)

Long-distance Paths of England and Wales, T.G. Millar (David & Charles)

The North Downs Way, H.D. Westacott (Penguin Books)

The Pilgrims' Way, Sean Jennett (Cassell)

The Pilgrims' Way and North Downs Way, C.J. Wright (Constable)

Ramblers' Ways, ed. David Sharp (David & Charles)

The Saxon Shore Way, Alan Sillitoe (Hutchinson)

The Thames Valley Heritage Walk, Miles Jebb (Constable)

Walkers' Britain (Pan Books)

Walks in Ashdown Forest and Around Tunbridge Wells, Hilary Longley-Cook (Waterdown Press, Frant)

Woodland Walks, Gerald Wilkinson (Webb & Bower). One comprehensive volume covers Britain's most interesting woodlands but is also issued in six separate regional volumes, including one for South-East England.

Publications in conjunction with the National Trust

Countryside Walks Series, ed. Steve Parker (Octopus)

  Home Counties

  Thames Valley and Cotswolds

Long Walks, Adam Nicolson (Weidenfeld & Nicolson)

The National Trust Guide, Rosemary Joekes and Robin Fedden (Cape)

Handbook of National Trust Properties Open (National Trust)

Properties of the National Trust, National Trust. (Includes details of estates and open spaces.)

General

English Heritage Guide (Historic Buildings & Monuments Commission)
From London for the Day, Carole Robson (Unwin Paperbacks)
Stately Homes, Museums, Castles and Gardens (Automobile Association)
The Woodland Trust Book of British Woodlands, Michael Allaby (David & Charles)

County and regional studies

Berkshire, Roger Higham (Batsford)
Portrait of Buckinghamshire, John Camp (Robert Hale)
Portrait of Epping Forest, Sir William Addison (Robert Hale)
Essex, Marcus Crouch (Batsford)
Portrait of Hertfordshire, Brian J. Bailey (Robert Hale)
Kent, Marcus Crouch (Batsford)
Middlesex, Bruce Steventon (Batsford)
Portrait of Surrey, Basil Cracknell (Robert Hale)
Sussex, John Burke (Batsford)

Tourist Information Centres

A number of the country parks and picnic sites dealt with in this book provide their own information boards and maps near the entrance or at strategic points. For the driver wanting comprehensive details of a site or additional interesting features in the near neighbourhood before setting out or while touring, local Tourist Information Centres carry a wide range of maps and leaflets, many of them free, and they can answer questions on the spot.

The following list of such Centres has been divided to fit in with the appropriate chapters. Inevitably this leads to a small amount of overlapping, since some counties and local administrations spread across more than one division. Also, a few of the offices are beyond our chosen limits, but I have included them because of their helpful general coverage of the area concerned.

South-East

CANTERBURY, Kent. 13 Longmarket. (0227) 66567.

CRANBROOK, Kent. Vestry Hall, Stone Street. (0580) 712538.

FAVERSHAM, Kent. Fleur de Lis Heritage Centre, 13 Preston Street. (0795) 534542.

GRAVESEND, Kent. 10 Parrock Street. (0474) 337600.

GREENWICH, Greater London. Cutty Sark Gardens, Greenwich Pier. (01) 858-6376.

MAIDSTONE, Kent. Old Palace Gardens, Mill Street. (0622) 671361.

ROCHESTER, Kent. Eastgate Cottage, High Street. (0634) 43666.

SEVENOAKS, Kent. Bligh's Car Park. (0732) 450305.

TUNBRIDGE WELLS, Kent. Town Hall. (0892) 26121.

South

ASHDOWN FOREST, Sussex. Ashdown Forest Centre, Wych Cross. (Limited opening hours. Volunteer staff. Telephone enquiries not encouraged.)

CROYDON, Surrey. Katharine Street. (01) 688-3627.

KINGSTON-UPON-THAMES, Surrey. Heritage Centre, Fairfield West. (01) 546-5386.

LEWES, East Sussex. Lewes House, 32 High Street. (0273) 471600.

RICHMOND, Surrey. Central Library, Little Green. (01) 940-9125.

TWICKENHAM, Middlesex. District Library, Garfield Road. (01) 892-0032.

WALTON-ON-THAMES, Surrey. Town Hall, New Zealand Avenue. (0932) 228844.

South-West

CHICHESTER, West Sussex. St Peter's Market, West Street. (0243) 775888.

FARNBOROUGH, Hampshire. County Library, Pinehurst Avenue. (0252) 513838.

FARNHAM, Surrey. Locality Office, South Street. (04868) 4104.

GUILDFORD, Surrey. Civic Hall, London Road. (0483) 575857.

PETERSFIELD, Hampshire. The Library, 27 The Square. (0730) 63451.

West

BRACKNELL, Berkshire. Central Library, Town Square. (0344) 423149.

HENLEY-ON-THAMES, Oxfordshire. Town Hall, Market Place. (0491) 578034.

MAIDENHEAD, Berkshire. Central Library, St Ives Road. (0628) 781110.

READING, Berkshire. Civic Offices, Civic Centre (0734) 592388.

WINDSOR, Berkshire. Central Station, Thames Street. (07535) 52010.

North-West

AMPTHILL, Bedfordshire. 12 Dunstable Street. (0525) 402051.

AYLESBURY, Buckinghamshire. County Hall, Walton Street. (0296) 5000.

BERKHAMSTED, Hertfordshire. Berkhamsted Library, Kings Road. (04427) 4545.

DUNSTABLE, Bedfordshire. The Library, Vernon Place. (0582) 608441.

HIGH WYCOMBE, Buckinghamshire. Council Offices, Queen Victoria Road. (0494) 26100.

RICKMANSWORTH, Hertfordshire. 17-23 High Street. (0923) 776611.

North

BOREHAMWOOD, Hertfordshire. Civic Offices, Elstree Way. (01) 207-2277.

EPPING FOREST, Essex. Queen Elizabeth's Hunting Lodge and Museum, Rangers Road, Chingford. (01) 508-2266. (Also information, maps and booklets at Epping Forest Conservation Centre, High Beach. (01) 508-7714.)

HEMEL HEMPSTEAD, Hertfordshire. The Pavilion, Marlowes. (0442) 64451.

HERTFORD, Hertfordshire. Vale House, 43 Cowbridge. (0279) 5526.

HITCHIN, Hertfordshire. Hitchin Library, Paynes Park. (0462) 34738.

LEE VALLEY PARK, Essex/Hertfordshire/Middlesex. Most of the individual sites described in this book have their own offices and tourist material, but for general enquiries regarding the whole complex the head office is at Lee Valley Park, Myddelton House, Bulls Cross, Enfield, Middlesex EN2 9HG: (0992) 717711. For a 24-hour information service, (0992) 761333.

ST ALBANS, Hertfordshire. 37 Chequer Street. (0799) 24282.

STEVENAGE, Hertfordshire. Central Library, Southgate. (0438) 69441.

WELWYN GARDEN CITY, Hertfordshire. The Campus. (07073) 31212.

North-East

BISHOP'S STORTFORD, Hertfordshire. Council Offices, The Causeway. (0279) 55261.

BRENTWOOD, Essex. Essex County Council Parks Office, Weald Park, South Weald Country Park, near Brentwood. Enquiries, and bookings for conducted tours with a parks warden, Brentwood (0277) 216297.

COLCHESTER, Essex. Town Hall, High Street. (0206) 46379.

DEDHAM, Essex. Dedham Vale Countryside Centre, Duchy Barn, The Drift. (0206) 323447

MALDON, Essex. 2 High Street. (0621) 56503.

SAFFRON WALDEN, Essex. Corn Exchange, Market Square. (0799) 24282.

INDEX

The abbreviation CP indicates a Country Park, PS a Picnic Site